A Year of Tiramisu

L.J. Brown

A Year of Tiramisu

Based on a true story

Chimera

A CIP catalogue record for this title is
available from the British Library.

ISBN 978 1 903136 63 8

Chimera is an imprint of
Pegasus Elliot MacKenzie Publishers Ltd.
www.pegasuspublishers.com

The author has tried to recreate events, locales and conversations from her
memories of them. In order to maintain their anonymity in some instances
she has changed the names of individuals and places. She may have
changed some identifying characteristics and details such as physical
properties, occupations and places of residence.

First Published in 2018
Chimera
Sheraton House Castle Park
Cambridge England

Printed & Bound in Great Britain

Dedication

To my publisher for hopefully funding my divorce, from the sales of this book.

To my f*ck buddy. I don't think heaven will let me in after writing this book, but I will meet you again one day, and we can make some magic happen amongst the stars.

To my friends who have put up with me and my love life for the last twelve months, you all deserve a medal.

And of course…for tiramisu and wine…

Warning

I wrote this book when I was bored, a little pissed and extremely horny.

I would advise you NOT to read this book IF:

1. You don't have a sense of humour
2. You have a heart condition as some content is shocking
3. You don't have an open mind
4. You are prepared to die from laughing
5. You do NOT want to get turned on
6. You are an extreme feminist

Preface
A Year of Tiramisu

What is the world coming to? At breakfast this morning, yet again another naughty pic sent to me on Messenger; this must be the second this week. I do feel a bit bad that I thought it was a potato and actually asked him why he was sending me a photo of a strangely shaped vegetable. I guess I won't hear from "Mr Manofyourdreams1234" again.

Not a great start to the day. I was waiting in the train station with a coffee, and I had an 'I'm worth it' moment in front of a very attractive man. Tossing my hair to one side, one of my hair extensions fell out onto the platform, right in front of him. God I can't believe I picked it up; it looked like a dead rat! Moment of sexy flirting brought to an abrupt end! Why do things like this happen to me?

Another disastrous date last night – I absolutely can't believe that such a successful businessman could do a thing like that. I mean COME ON, our first date and he has his pants down under the restaurant table and puts my hand on his surprisingly large penis. Thank God for wine, fire escapes and lots of SOAP!

No word from 'Mr Fancy Pants'. It's been almost two weeks now since our last crazy night of sex on his kitchen table. God I miss him; no idea why, I'm totally 'Little Miss Dial A Shag'. I should hate him.

Nineteen dates now! WHERE IS HE? I'm so fed up. I need my tiramisu and wine!

One thousand and twenty messages to reply to on POF, something to do before I fall asleep, perhaps I should hire a PA? No date for the weekend so far; not sure if I should pay my gas bill or get a spray tan just in case?

Chapter One
Can't Get No Satisfaction

I know that keeping a journal of all your thoughts and feelings can really help with emotional upset in life. This is the first time I've ever really been single, therefore I've decided to keep a log book next to my bed so that I don't torture myself emotionally. I'm not holding back anything; I'm going to say it how it is, as it happens... it will be very therapeutic I think? First entry tonight.

Single life starts in the shower. It's my very first weekend on my own without the kids, after leaving my husband. It's the evening and I'm drained from the split up, so I think I deserve to get totally pissed!

Nothing planned other than unpacking boxes and trying to keep a smile on my face. God, it's really hit me. I'm on my own; what the hell do I do with myself? I feel like I miss him, like I've made a mistake, but he's a complete d*ck and I'm well rid of him. I'm sure these are natural detachment feelings. Think of him as a toilet brush! Keep thinking that!

I had a shower for over an hour, washing in my ex-husband's shower gel just so I could feel close to him. I'm the one who left him, silly cow. BIN IT tomorrow, I don't need any more reminders. I have to do something to stop myself feeling things for him; I can't go backwards, only forwards.

My play list was on my laptop and the song 'I can't get no satisfaction' was blaring out; God, I love the Rolling Stones.

Sod it; I'm taking my vibrator in for play.

Dancing round my room wet through, I go into my toy box and get out my rabbit. I only started getting a collection of toys a few months ago after chatting to 'Mr Under The Table'. Now there's a man I can think about in the shower. Fit, sexy, hairy gym buddy. God, he turns me on. Can't believe we have spent so much time together and not had sex.

'I can't get no satisfaction' is the perfect song to do this to, not had a shag in so long that this is the best I can do/hope for right now. I put the song on repeat, downed a glass of wine and got back in.

The wine went to my head quickly, I must remember to eat. Repeating to myself I'm single, washing my long hair and tossing it about to the music. I'M SINGLE, I'M SINGLE, I'M SINGLE until I could really hear it in my head. It's REAL!

Finally a wine induced massive grin of achievement crossed my face: I did it. I left the f*cker. I'm proud of myself. NO MORE TEARS, he's made me cry enough and I don't look pretty when I cry, only when I cry out in pleasure!

Using the vibrator as a microphone I belt out the song, dancing around being as silly and as loud as I can. There's no one here to stop me, MY HOUSE, MY TIME, MY VIBRATOR, MY NEW LIFE!

After a couple of rounds of Rolling Stones and having lots of play time I get out and wrap myself in a towel, fall face planting the floor falling over my own feet pissed, but still find it funny.

I have to do something with my time tonight, make it special; this is a new day in my life. All my friends have told me to sign up to a dating site; I can't imagine it will be any good though. I've only ever had two boyfriends and one I married, and both times I've been pulled, not the other way round. I have never had to look. This should be interesting, always good to learn new things? Right?

Since I'm pissed and naked, perhaps this is the best time to have to take the plunge. POF, AKA Plenty Of Fish, funny name but I get where it's coming from, plenty more d*ckheads in the sea maybe?

I logged on and it asked me for my details and photos, so I had to pick out my best selfies, and a sexy full body shot. I'm quite confident about my body and the way I look; yes I have hair extensions but other than that and a fake tan (which I only get because I'm so pale), I'm very real and quite natural looking. I tried the fake eyelashes once and ended up swallowing one in my tea, not for me!

I'm an average, not unattractive young lady I think? Perhaps the wine is making me slightly over confident. I put a photo on of me in a short and sexy red dress at Christmas, with my very long legs out, and a few close ups and a side shot.

My profile: at first I wrote the truth, and then did a lot of deleting. It's like drink texting, you always regret it.

*'Desperate, attention seeking single mother, who has not had a f*ck in over a year due to d*ckhead ex-husband's boredom and looking elsewhere. In need of a real man, with a bit of attitude and sense of humour, someone to f*ck me stupid and take me out for an expensive steak.'*

That should do it but I have to lie to attract the 'right' attention?

Hey there…

'I've only been single a short time after a marriage split, and don't really know what to put. First time on here. I'm a nice down-to-earth mum of two; perhaps we could chat and then maybe go for a glass of wine or six? Message me if you like my profile.'

Down to earth? Ha, crazy as a box of frogs, not of this world, perhaps an alien sent down to earth on a mission to f*ck up? Definitely on a mission to have a f*ck, at some point at least.

How depressing. Society has put me here. I have to resort to online dating, how SAD is this? I feel so drunk and sorry for myself. I have no one to go to sleep with tonight, no one to cuddle, no one to talk to and my house, apart from the cat, is so silent.

I'm quite scared. I don't like this need for someone in my life. I'm not used to being on my own. I need to cry, I need to cry a lot.

I'm even scared of the dark and can't have the lights out, got emergency candles in my room by my bed just in case of a power cut.

What if I never have sex again? What will happen to me? Will my lady bits actually stop working? Big 'out of order' sign. Do not enter, not been used in over a year, might contain explosives, deemed a danger, enter at your peril!

Right. I've submitted it to the stupid dating website, let's see what happens.

Grabbing my pillows and lining them up like a body so it feels like someone's with me, I take my last swig of wine and pass out.

Chapter Two
'The Leprechaun'

I've been talking to two men on POF after creating my profile a few days ago. An Irish man who seems amazing in every respect, he ticks all the boxes, and some guy who lives not far away, who has been supportive somewhat and is very fit, but obviously putting younger photos of himself online. You can tell he's older and slightly boring, and he doesn't believe that my profile pics are me? I think that's a bit rude, it most definitely is me, just because I do look younger than I am and have a good body I'm instantly a fake profile? He won't even meet me in a public place because he's had bad dates in the past with people who turn up slightly larger and definitely not the person on the profile pic. Shallow! But hey whatever, I don't think I want to meet him.

I've been getting some awful messages and seedy texts from random weirdos. I can't believe how many messages I've received in such a short space of time. Most of these people are not looking for dating, they just want sex. Have I signed up to the wrong website? It's free, I'm broke. It's going to have to do. Got a message from 'w*nkman123'. 'Hey, sexy, want to ride me tonight?' Errmm no thanks, I'd rather eat my own sh*t. BLOCK! The number of people on here who just say "Hi, how are you?" over and over again and having to reply to over a hundred of these a day gets so DULL. No profiles, no information about the person. Do any of you have a mind? Really want to talk?

My first date from a dating website is tonight. I was so impressed by his profile; it was like an essay, he had put massive effort into letting people know what he was all about and what he was looking for, obviously smart and funny. I understood that he was quirky right away. Scared of velvet however, little bit weird? I have to bring that up in conversation, I need to know more. I'm thinking coffins and that scares me.

What's on my mind most of all is that I have not had sex in months, and I have no idea what I'm doing or what I'm going to say or even do if we decided to have sex. I don't even know if I'm good at it. I have shaved my bits thoroughly just in case, although we both said first date, no sex! I'm taking a massive risk too; we've been talking for a few days and it's been so much fun, but I don't know him. I've never known anyone so funny who understands my sense of humour, this is a big deal for me. He's had me crying with laughter and we have talked on the phone for hours. Sexting a little but not too much, RESPECT! His voice has me weak at my knees. Irish sexy f*cker! He's sent me voice recordings on WhatsApp and I've been playing them back over and over, listening to him. I love his voice. So, we flipped a coin, heads he comes to my place, tails we don't meet totally up to fate. We did it live so we could both see what happened over the phone, it was heads! The luck of the Irish!

The doorbell rang. I'd already had a bottle of wine to steady my nerves. When he walked through my doorway, tall and handsome and full of smiles, I didn't know what had hit me. He didn't look like his profile pic, he was more attractive; I'd never seen such a handsome man. We awkwardly said hello and walked into the kitchen with the wine he had brought, which had a bull on the cork, I hoped this was an omen. He took the piss out of the paintings on my fridge that the kids had done, knowing I was an artist, he tried to compliment me on my work. It was a great ice breaker; he was very funny. We sat in my front room for hours, drinking wine and talking.

He then reached over to kiss me and a current of electricity ran through my blood, it was pure lust. I stood up, told him I was going to go take my contact lenses out and I wouldn't be coming back downstairs, dropping my clothes to the floor bit by bit on the way up.

I waited for him in bed, I wasn't scared the wine and lust had taken over and I felt brave. I had to take the plunge at some point and sleep with someone new. After twelve years of one man, a new chapter is opening up, as well as my long legs. Holy shit balls! He came in the room and dropped his pants 'Leprechauns' are massive, it's a myth that they are 'tiny'; how's that going to fit! Swinging it around to the music and dancing round the room, I couldn't think of having sex for laughing.

I ordered him to dress up in my stockings and suspenders, and dance round my bedroom doing the River dance. I have never laughed so hard in my life, he owned it, and he looked good for a man. Definitely could audition for Rocky Horror.

We made love for hours after that, and everything was OK until I called him by his name during sex – he suddenly stopped; he said that that actually wasn't his real name. I was in shock, pissed shock, but still shock and quickly got off him. Flashing his driving licence at me, he told me his real name. I said WTF, why would he need to fake-name me? I've just slept with him. What's going on? Is he married? Does he have a girlfriend? Panic set in. What if he's a convicted murderer, or a stalker, or like Dexter? My thoughts were running wild. He's in my house. I just wanted him to go home after that. Stupid, STUPID girl!

I called him after he'd gone home and the number was no longer in use. OH MY GOD. I've been used by a cross dressing leprechaun psychopath. First date, what the hell am I letting myself in for? Then a mixture of guilt and depression set in, I had just slept with someone other than my husband, and I'm still married. SIN, I'm going to burn in HELL!

Chapter Three
Laxatives

On and off I have been chatting to boring 'Mr. Fancy Pants' on POF. I call him this because he shows off about his fancy life a lot. Not sure I'm very excited about meeting him on our first date tonight and I've already tried to get out of it, but he's keen, even called me from his work phone and asked me if I'm going. He's picked up the vibe and I feel a bit sorry for him so I'm going to go, my heart's not in it though.

I spent all day trying to find something to wear, my unpacking's still not done and I can't find anything. I said I'd wear a little black dress and heels but I've changed my mind because he's not made me feel all that sexy. I need a more casual look for the first date; it's his house I'm going to, since he doesn't want to meet me in public, and he still doesn't believe I'm not nineteen stone and look like the elephant man.

A few hours before I was due to go I had a small glass of wine for courage and my tummy started to make some very funny sounds. I rushed to the loo and had a bad bout of the runs, it was GREEN. I thought I was going to die! Then I remembered, I took laxatives twenty-four hours ago so that my tummy would be nice and flat before my date. Not that I was planning to show him my tummy or any part of me.

Two hours to go before the date, I have to drive there and use my sat nav for the first time to find his posh house in the middle of nowhere, what am I going to do? I can't go to his house and shit everywhere. What happens if it runs down my legs? Every possible situation went through my head.

Emergency call to Gem!

"Gemma, I've got the sh*ts and I have to go on this date tonight, what do I do?"

After listening to her laugh for about ten minutes when I'd gone into details that it was green and smelt worse than my cooking, she advised me to sit on the loo till it had passed and take something to stop the runs.

After a while, it reduced but I felt a bit sick, I might shit myself and throw up in his mouth now! This is going to be the date from hell.

I wore a long sexy dress with pretty flowers on it and heels. I'd had a spray tan and my hair extensions had recently been done and looked full and lush. Apart from having to hold my bum cheeks in, I looked good enough for at least a snog, if I liked him and he liked me.

I dropped in at the shop for a bottle of red as a kind gesture and hoped that he had lots more.

I had set up my sat navigation then got my phone to type in the postal code he had sent me but unable to find his text message with his address on. Double shit, I'm late and now I have to phone him and ask him for his address again. This is NOT going well.

'Mr Fancy Pants' answered the phone; I think he was expecting me to cancel. I said I was sorry but I'd deleted his text by mistake and was going to need it again, and might possibly be a few minutes late. I could tell he was thinking that I was useless, he'd better not get his fancy knickers in a twist or I won't turn up; he was a bit short with me. Why the hell am I going? With any luck, I will shit everywhere – serves him right.

Holding my bum cheeks in and taking a deep breath, I set off. My music was belting out full blast and it felt like my stomach was settling down, but then my nerves kicked in and I felt sick again. What if he doesn't like me, what if I don't look OK, what the hell do I say to him? My phone rang when I was nearly there and it was 'Mr Star Wars' so I pulled over and took the call. I couldn't have been far away, maybe only five minutes and I was not very late, thank goodness. 'Mr Star Wars' wanted the address of where I was going and the name of the person I was going on the date with, just in case I was murdered and never seen again. He's such a good friend, definitely boyfriend material but as we had reached that 'friend zone', he was now the person I called about my dates, all the disasters and advice on clothes and sex.

The main bit of advice was not to sleep with him, keep it cool and don't talk too much. I can do that. I'm not even sure why I'm going, other than it's my weekend off and I have nothing better to do. I had two emergency energy-boosting cans of Red Bull and I drank them quickly while I was talking to him. The sat navigation said I was five minutes away from 'Mr Fancy Pants' millionaire house.

After going round in circles for almost ten minutes, I was now very late and I had to pull over and call him again, lost and needing a pee! He actually said I was useless at the end of the telephone conversation, great start to the date. I took his instructions, turned left at the shop and I drove down a long drive way. Holy f*ck, he lives in a mansion. He had seen my car and called me again, telling me I was in the wrong parking space, making me feel stupid AGAIN. I moved my car and pulled up outside his house.

Swapping my flats for heels, I got out of the car, shutting the door on my hair extensions thereby pulling a few out, and he was watching out of the window – great look! Lost three times, parked in the wrong place and now look like a screwed up mess attached to my car by my hair!

I'm almost tripping over on the gravel to his house, with a bottle of wine in my hands, putting the wine before my safety I stumbled forward to his door and knocked. He opened the door with a half-smile, a worried look that said everything – 'what the f*ck have I let myself in for!' The only thing I could think of was that I needed the toilet so badly. I smiled and tried to be as confident as I could.

He was wearing a white shirt and jeans, had dark hair and beautiful brown eyes. I handed him the bottle of wine and he smiled and invited me in. I felt nothing, other than 'OMG he's quite a bit older than me', and 'shit he's loaded'. No immediate attraction; this was going to be a long night.

Standing in his kitchen, he reached for some glasses and opened the wine, filled our glasses and we chatted about my navigational skills, or lack of them. Taking the piss out of me but he was so confident and relaxed that he put me at ease. I think he could tell I was a bit scared. We took the wine to the sofa, a long, black, leather, three quarter sofa that could fit at least eight people. He sat about as far away from me as he could and vice versa. I didn't dare ask for the loo so I crossed my legs and waited until I was desperate. The Red Bull I'd had whilst parked up hit me and I started to feel giddy, so decided what the hell, in a situation like this, all I can do is get wasted and hope for the best. It will be a fun taxi ride home!

I talked for ages, quite fast and he listened to me. I covered most of my education, work and hobbies, my family and my friends and tried to be funny and sexy at the same time. He looked positively bored and didn't say much so I asked him questions and his answers were dull. He didn't want to give anything away. His name sounded slightly foreign and when he told me what his last name was I completely forgot it almost immediately so he spelt it out but it did not compute.

Suddenly I started to find him quite sexy, perhaps it was because he wasn't showing much interest in me or that I liked his fancy house, definitely his taste in art. I felt it might be a good idea to move closer to him so I asked to use the loo, luckily I didn't have an accident on the way and came back to sit closer. I sat right next to him, playing with my hair, giving off the signals to him that I quite fancied him and that I wanted him to make a move or to kiss me. He wasn't going to do anything, he looked awkward. I could smell his aftershave and it sent me wild. I love a man who smells and dresses smartly; it didn't matter that he had a bit of grey hair and no personality. Looking into his eyes I made a move, I dared to kiss him. I kissed him hard and deep and wanted him to grab me and want me back, so why is he still holding back? No sex on the first date was the rule for tonight but we were both quite drunk by now and I was feeling super turned on by him, something was going to happen, and I definitely can't drive home now.

'Mr Star Wars' advice about not getting drunk or talking too much had both gone out of the window and now I wanted sex too.

Reaching over to the side table, I tried to put my wine glass down but it fell off, smashing all over the floor. Wine and glass everywhere, I got up and dashed to clean it up but he stopped me and told me off, making sure I didn't cut myself. Again that look of 'WTF have I got into here?' came across his face. Cleaning up the spilt wine and broken glass and me apologising constantly, the sexy mood had dissipated, and I needed the loo because I was feeling ill again.

Going into the bathroom, I shut the door and rushed to the loo. It was massive and beautiful bathroom; I loved his house, even though it was in a mess because he was moving.

I sat down on the loo and gave out a massive fart. F*CK! I hope he didn't hear that. Jesus! Luckily the runs had stopped and I was in the clear, no green poo. But OMG I can't leave the room, he must have heard that. F*CK! F*CK! F*CK! I stayed in the loo for about ten minutes and gave myself a talking to.

Applying some lipstick, and talking to myself in the mirror I decided, what the hell, you only live once. Surprisingly, I fancy him, he might not fancy me but if I have sex tonight, I have sex. It's not like I'm ever going to see this man again, I have already worked out he's not that interested, and this won't last.

Confident in the thought that I wouldn't sh*t myself and that hopefully with the music being on downstairs, this had masked my massive fart, I walked down the stairs and into the kitchen where he was pouring a fresh glass of wine for me, after clearing up. He told me I owed him a very expensive wine glass and to be careful with the next one or he'd be getting me a plastic cup for the next time I came over. Next time, he wants me to come back after all this?

We sat down on the sofa, got close and we kissed long and hard and pushed into each other, and then started to undress each other slowly. He definitely hadn't heard my explosive fart. To my amazement, he kissed better than I'd ever been kissed before. He was good, better than good – absolutely amazing.

His top was off, good God he was so hairy, it was everywhere, he was like a monkey. I liked it, and he felt so warm and smelt SO good on top of me. Kissing me he said, "I guess the no sex on the first date agreement is out of the window then?" I shrugged my shoulders and let him carry on. Oh my, this man has surprised me. 'Mr Fancy Pants', dull as f*ck, has turned into a sex machine. Putting his fingers inside me, he did something I've never experienced before. I felt like I was going to explode, he did it so fast and with such skill. Pulling me up he took my hand and said, "Let's go to bed."

I was freezing, shaking with a mixture of being scared and so turned on, he sat me on the bed, pushed me down and went down on me, playing with me for what felt like forever. I had never had so much attention; he was not selfish at all. Then he was inside me and watching me, like he was searching for me to reassure him that I liked what he was doing. Oh I liked it, I liked it a lot. He made me cum over and over again until I felt like I was going to faint, different positions and lots of kissing, really attentive. My last two partners didn't last as long as the Countdown clock and it's over and done with.

We cuddled up, I knocked over another glass of wine and he got pissed off with me. As I was too pissed to care and too sleepy from sex, I told him to stop moaning on, and surprised that I wasn't thrown out. Lying next to each other in the dark, we talked about relationships. I said I was at that point in my life where I didn't want anything or at least wasn't sure what I was looking for. Everything had been so awful before and I wanted to explore my new found single life. Both of us were on the exact same page. This was, or could potentially be, pretty awesome.

I think we only got an hour's sleep, but when we woke up, he said, "Are you still here? You need to go, I have my kids coming over soon."

I went to the bathroom feeling quite pissed off and thought I might slap him when I returned to his bedroom. Falling over all the clothes on his floor, I gathered up my things and as I was leaving, he put the pillow over his head and said I could let myself out. I hate him, 'Mr Fancy Pants Wanker F*ck-Face' and I will NEVER let myself see him again!

Driving home I realised that it had just been a one-night stand and that I didn't like him. He was handsome and I liked the sex, it had been fun, but I wouldn't allow myself to feel like that again. He really upset me.

Sh*t – I have left my underwear!

Chapter Four
Cucumber Practice

Lights are dimmed, candles are lit and the wine is flowing. 'Fifty Shades' sound track is playing in the background. The mood is set.

Placing a very large cucumber on the bed and two small oranges, I visualise a man on my bed. I'm going to pretend that someone is there, watching me take my clothes off. I start to do a sexy dance and slowly start to strip to the Rolling Stones' song 'Beast of Burden'. I let my hair down and drink a sip of my wine, tossing my hair around slowly. I kick my high-heels off; now I undo the first suspender, then the next, and then slowly roll my knickers down my long legs. Bra slowly coming off, I swing it in the air and throw it on the bed, knocking the cucumber away from the oranges; drat – I've broken my pretend penis already.

Naked, I kneel on the bed and try to focus. I can do this, I like cucumber, I have it in my sandwiches ALL the time, it tastes good – stay focused and lick the cucumber! Running my tongue all the way up the cucumber, I close my eyes and think of what a man would want me to do to him at this point. I put my hand underneath the cucumber and open my eyes, staring at my pillow where he'd be watching me. Slowly, I put the cucumber inside my mouth and start to take it, slowly and as fully as I can without gagging, caressing the oranges and squeezing them. God, it feels hard inside my mouth, I must be doing a good job. I squeeze one of the oranges too hard and juice goes all over my hand, pre-cum already – nice touch.

This cucumber is getting bigger and bigger in my mouth. What's going on? It's growing, FAST! I can't fit this in for much longer. HELP, this is scaring me, I will have to try to bite it to stop it growing any bigger but I don't want to hurt my cucumber.

Biting the cucumber's end off, it explodes everywhere, all over the room and my face, and then I wake up.

Looking around my room for traces of cucumber, still half asleep. Since I met 'Fancy Pants' all I do is think and dream about SEX, what has this man done to me, and why does my subconscious have to point out all the things I'm worried about in bed?

Chapter Five
Naked Dancing

Awful day, my kids hate me, my job's crap and on my Friday night off, no one's playing out.

I have NO date and 34p in the bank. I have to make my own happiness tonight again. I'm going to have to be creative with my evening, drink some wine and have food and do something different. I hate watching crap TV and movies, such a waste of life. I've read all my books twice and can't really afford to go out and buy a good book when I have priorities (fake tan and hair extensions); oh and that bloody gas bill.

Bills bills bills. BIN BIN BIN!

Went to the shop and bought a litre bottle of vodka, making me go over my limit on my account, but I needed it. I will sort that problem out later. I'm sure this bad boy will last me a month, a little dash of orange juice and a portion of my favourite cake, tiramisu. Perfect. This is officially my LONELY ritual.

The kids have smashed all the decent glassware, so I'm drinking out of a mug saying 'Best mum in the world'. Whatever, worst mum in the world more like; I'm so sick of being in the bad books. When did they decide to turn from sweet little darlings into hormonal nightmares? I love them but I'm so glad of my own space.

I decided to move all my furniture around in my bedroom so that I had a dance floor, and adjusted the lights so they pointed towards one area of the room. I created a pretend dance floor tonight.

I'm going to try on everything I have of my clothes and have a good chuck out of things that remind me of my past with my ex, anything I've been keeping hold of that makes me look like a total mess or everything that will continue to work for me in the future – AKA pulling clothes. Booming out music and emptying the entire contents of my wardrobe onto the bed, I throw back a full cup of vodka and pour myself another.

Naked apart from a thong, I look in the mirror. God my body has changed! I'm so skinny, no fat on me anywhere; all those hours in the gym chasing after 'Mr Under The Table' have paid off. Hair down to my bottom, wavy and shiny, and even without make up on I feel sexy. My boobs have shrunk and look a little different in shape, better I think, but definitely smaller. My flat, toned stomach has line definition and my thong hangs on my hips, like a sexy handbag hangs on my arm.

Drinking vodka, Pink blasts out on the play list and 'Try' comes on. I start to dance round my little spotlight stage, kicking my high-heels out of the way, taking my knickers off and throwing them at my mirror. I put on my sexiest pair of black stilettos and start to dance. Naked dancing is the future; it's a therapy all on its own. Watching myself in the mirror, and tossing my hair around to the music, I feel as free as a bird. There is a little bit of magic in this room tonight, no man or batteries included.

I kneel down in front of my mirror, grab one of my breasts, and point it at the mirror like a loaded gun; shoot and wink, then blow the smoke away. I then continue to dance like a crazy person, giggling due to the alcohol, and singing at the top of my voice. I was mid flow when all the lights went out. I hate the dark – this was my worst nightmare. Pissed and naked, I try to find my phone to get the torch to work. Falling over everything in my high-heels and knocking my drink over, and finally find it, I use the light from it to go downstairs and check the mains. The street is in darkness, not just my house. I was not impressed; I was having such a good night too.

Scared, I climb into bed and pull the covers over my head and go on Facebook to see what's going on; the town was in darkness. What's going on? It's naked dancing night.

I messaged 'Mr Under The Table'; he always answers me and helps me get to sleep no matter what he's doing. 'Hey, bit dark isn't it?'

'Evening, yeah it's not good, have you got some candles?'

'Me and candles...you kidding? House would probably be set on fire, but yeah I do have some, just under my sheets hiding from the boogeyman.'

'Haha. True.'

'So, it's late, you in bed?'

'No I'm sitting in front to the TV in the dark. What have you been up to tonight then?'

'It's my weekend off; I've got pissed and danced around my bedroom naked, to loud music.'

'Haha, not like you? No dates, no fella? What's happened to that Mr Fancy Pants you had a date with?'

'Well I went on a date to his house, he didn't want to be seen with me in public. I got a bit drunk and did the wrong thing. Sex on the first date. Ooops!'

'Was it any good?'

'He was different.'

'It's not a crime to have sex on the first date you know, most people do these days.'

'I know, it's just I've done it twice in a row now and I'm feeling a bit slutty.'

'You shouldn't feel shit, you're HOT and SINGLE!'

'You still fancy me, Mr, don't you? I miss meeting up with you in the gym.'

'I miss making you cum and pulling your bikini off in the swimming pool!'

'I miss you making me cum too. I can't believe we have never had sex.'

'I'm spoken for, we can't can we?'

'I know, you're my best mate and my cum buddy, you feeling a bit frisky now? Take your pants off I want to see him, I've missed him SO much.'

'I'm not hard.'

'Well remember the time I took all my clothes off in the car park at the gym, and how much that turned you on? Everyone able to see us?'

'LMAO. HOW could I EVER forget that, little Miss Naughty? Little bit of movement going on now…'

'Now close your eyes and play with it, remembering me sucking it in the steam room, jacuzzi, sauna and pool.'

'F*ck, that was HOT. Mmmm, I'm HARD as f*ck.'

'Show me!' I got a picture of his penis by candle light, it was very hard and I was instantly turned on. A full year of messing around and never having sex was extremely frustrating but had kept it alive. This is how we got our kicks, only they had been getting less and less frequent as it was coming to an end. We were going back into the friends zone and he was definitely never going to leave his partner for me.

'I want you to wank off, film it and send it to me.'

'I will do it if you do it too.'

'OK, you go first.'

'If I was there right now, I would throw you down on the bed and f*ck you so hard, with your legs around my neck and smacking that sweet little bottom of yours…'

'Would you now, would you kiss me hard?' I had to light a few candles to be able to see what I was doing, sexting by candle light was certainly new for us.

'Yeah, I'd bite your lip and make it bleed I'd kiss you that hard, God I want you. I want to watch your boobs bouncing around while I f*ck you hard and fast. Then I'd bite them too, lick your nipples.'

'Mr Under The Table, are you hungry? Do you need to go make a sandwich and continue?'

'Lol, stop talking and start playing.'

'I'm so wet right now; you've made me so ready. I want your head between my legs, making me scream for you to stop. I'm playing, don't worry, was doing before we even started this conversation. FACE TIME ME.'

Both of us get on the phone and watch each other play for about five minutes, hear each other cum, blow each other a virtual kiss, give each other a cheeky grin and hang up, exhausted.

I text him, 'We are a right pair of wankers, you know! Wink! Good night, I love ya, hahahahahh'

'Goodnight, love you too. x'

Chapter Six
Marriage Should Be Made Illegal

I woke up to a message from 'Mr Under The Table', explaining that he felt guilty and that our relationship had to stop.

My earliest memory of him was me sliding down a bannister at nursery age three and it making my 'Mary Jane' as I called it back then, give a little 'tingling'. I grabbed his hand and told him that my heart beat had moved and to feel it beating. He told me to slide down the bannister again and again to see how fast we could get it to beat in-between my legs. It was our little game, it was fun, but he couldn't recall it when we started talking dirty to each other in our late 30s. He did remember under the table though. We had just got married in dressing up clothes and we are celebrating by having our first kiss hidden away under a tablecloth at the back of the church hall. We slobbered all over each other and he was pulling at his pants. I asked what he was doing and he said his 'soldier' felt funny. I went out from under the table and came back with a plastic first aid kit and began to do all sort of examinations to his penis, finally putting it in a bandage and telling him he would be fine.

We didn't see each other after nursery, until I walked into a classroom of boys at sixth form. He was sitting at the desk opposite me; we looked at each other in shock and laughed out loud, what a blast from the past. I was sixteen, now had boobs and wore make up and he was a scruffy mess and spotty. He had a girlfriend and I had a really bad crush on an older man with a car, so we were friends again but like passing ships.

Another twelve years went by and I literally bumped into him in the street whilst taking my kids to school and not looking where I was going. We looked at each other and we both gave a massive smile, but couldn't place each other. Later that day I had a message on Facebook from him asking if it was me who he'd seen in the street. We then realised we both have been living in the same town for the past seven years and not known, and the rest is history.

We finished it today and it made me reflect so much. I promised him that I would go on as many dates as I could, to find 'the one', and as my best mate in the world he would always be there for me, to listen and hug me if I needed him. This ended in the best possible and kindest way and I know I will always love him.

Under firm instruction, I logged back onto the dating sites, but my heart was a little sore, I would miss him.

I'd had so many conversations trying to find a date, ended up counselling half of them and getting the other half back with their partners. I had one conversation tonight with a man that became quite heated, about marriage. He confused the heck out of me with his bullshit. We ended up telling each other to f*ck off and then he sent me a picture of his penis. I blocked him, looked up at my ceiling and thought I was going to be alone for the rest of my life.

Then I thought to myself, do I really want to be sitting in a nursing home at ninety years old with the same f*cking person who pisses me off 99.9% of the time? Not being able to get out of my chair to f*ck off out and leave them when they are talking shit? The best I could hope for is shitting myself and telling them that they will have to wipe my bottom to get them to piss off and ask for help, no, I have to find someone I would always get on with, someone that gets me, someone who would gladly wipe my ass!

I started remembering being at school and having that one subject which I just couldn't get my head round, it made no sense to me at all. Even when it was clearly explained to me over and over again, it simply didn't compute. In fact, it gave me a banging headache trying to work it out. Men do this to me. Men are a complicated mathematical equation that I can't solve. I couldn't do trigonometry at school; I hated maths, full stop. I wanted to understand things in a logical way, but it would end up as that big ball of confusion in my head and a lot of time wasted trying to figure out why I was even trying so hard to work something out that probably would have no representation in my life, no meaning and no reason for me learning it. To me, right now, marriage/relationships are just the same. A big f*ck off waste of time.

Yes, we all fall in love with someone, well, we think we do. We then get confused about who we are with, why we are with them and why we didn't stay single. Nearly all of us mess this up, not just once but over and over again. Then we start having children. Now we have two people who used to get on, but now can't wait to be apart from each other, but have children so they have to suffer each other's company even more.

Marriage is a main cause of depression, anxiety, sexual frustration, loss of self worth, alcoholism, drug abuse, cheating, lying and self-harm. Why do people still think it's a good idea? I will never EVER re-marry!

I think that the happiest people I know, just have casual relationships with someone they know they will have fun with and have amazing sex. It never gets dull then, never gets too serious and it brings out the best in them, because they have no anticipation to be something to someone.

We were born alone and naked. If we were supposed to have someone attached to us twenty-four hours a day, God would have glued us together, for f*ck's sake! I agree with the naked part.

No thanks, they should register a new vote in the general elections for marriage to be made illegal; it comes with a very serious health warning and divorce lawyers are making far too much money out of it.

F*ck buddies are the future!

Chapter Seven
Blow Jobs And Bottoms

Screw parents! I swear to God, if one of them turns round to me and says, "I told you so," or, "if you had just listened to me it would never have happened," I might actually divorce them.

My mum tells me I'm doing things wrong ALL the time, my dad sits silently until I ask him a direct question and then he gives me a very blunt answer, "Yes, your ex-husband was a complete and utter waste of space, and your life is a mess unless you do something to turn this around."

I'm not doing well in any aspect of my life right now; I think the company I'm working for is about to go bust, I'm in debt after my separation and hardly affording to eat and clothe myself and the kids. I've even had my bank card taken off me and replaced with a crappy 'cash withdrawals only' card, so I can't go over my limit any more by buying bottles of vodka to see me though my sadness when I'm on my own.

My car is unreliable and about to die on me and I spend most of my free time in a gym, punishing myself so hard to stay slim so that someone will at least look twice at me, but forgetting to eat. I'm a mess – a complete train wreck. I have NO idea what I'm doing or what direction to go in. I'm simply reacting to life, and being very impulsive.

Tonight is another example of my stupid behaviour. I was offered another date (if you can call going to his house for a shag a date), with 'Mr Fancy Pants'. I had been 'advised' by my close friends not to EVER go near him again after the first time I'd slept with him and recent textual events causing me insecurity and feelings of worthlessness and serious lack of control.

'What you up to tonight?'

'Well hello, I thought you'd fallen off the face of the earth! I'm home attempting to cook and failing, why?'

'Just wondered if you would like to come over and suck my cock?'

'Cock? What cock? Reaches for magnifying glass!'

'About eight-thirty, then?'

'Pushy t*at! I'm too busy draining vegetables.'

'I've got some vodka!'

'What time?'

'Ha, what do you have to wear that's sexy?'

'Well you tell me what would turn you on and I will see what I can do.'

'Stockings, suspenders, heels?'

'Yeah I have them, you going to let me keep them on?'

'I will have to take your knickers off.'

'Just tear them with your teeth?'

'Can you come sooner?'

'No, I have to shave first and do you EVER pay attention, I'm cooking! Hahaha.'

'What are you wearing right now?'

'Fancy pants, I'm not getting naked for you.'

'Send me a picture of your pussy.'

'You can't handle my pussy.'

'I already have!'

'Forgotten all about it, you must have been... well...'

'Bring your toys?'

'Really? Can you not just shag me and let's see what it's like when we are both not pissed off our faces?'

'Yeah, yeah. Just bring them.'

I stopped texting him and had such a massive smile on my face, this man really lights me up and makes me feel young again, and up to no good. I love the banter and I felt so excited about seeing him, it surprises me, I really didn't feel that much connection at first. I put some music on and danced round my bedroom with a cheeky glass of wine, and said to myself in the mirror, "I'm off for another epic fancy shag, I hope he does that amazing thing with his fancy fingers again," then headed for the shower.

As I was putting my stockings on and pulling them up my legs when I put my nail though one, it got a massive ladder and it looked completely rubbish. If I text him now and tell him I've had to wear something else, he might cancel and if I'm honest I really did need sex, it has been four weeks since I last slept with him, so I will have to improvise.

I turned up in a dark pink and black lacy basque and some tiny black hot pants and a pair of killer heels. It looked very sexy and I'd just had a spray tan so my legs looked amazing long and brown.

Last time I had been to his house, it was a bit of a disaster so I had to make sure I didn't nearly shit myself, smash wine glasses, or do giant farts. Perhaps if I like him this time , this excitement might turn into something a little bit more than f*ck buddies. I'm still not sure about him; he never tells me anything about himself so I feel like he's got some big secret, hiding something from me, something that's a big deal, like his name used to be Doris.

Arriving at his house and explaining what had happened with the stockings was funny. He laughed at what I'd turned up in. We always seem to have a really good laugh together. The memory of what had happened the last time we saw each other had faded and it was like we'd known each other such a long time, nothing bothered me with him this time, and I could completely be myself.

We drank and laughed and then I kissed him passionately whilst on the immense sofa that I remembered so well from last time. He was sitting down so I got on top of him, but kept talking total crap at the same time; he wanted me to shut up, but made it into a joke so I wasn't offended. I got off him (not quite drunk) and stripped off to the music that was playing on his TV. I then continued to dance round the room doing sexy little moves and giggling, spilling wine on his perfect cream carpet. He walked over to me, took the wine glass out of my hand and set it to one side, pulling me down slowly to the floor on top of him. We kissed hard, our bodies warm and my fake tan coming off onto his clothes, he said I smelt like biscuits.

I undressed him, watching him and paying attention to his every expression, trying to read his thoughts, what's going on in that fancy little mind of his, let me in. I kissed his lips, and then kissed his face and his neck and moved my lips all over his chest. Smelling his aftershave and feeling like I could hardly contain myself with lust. I loved his hairy chest – it sent me into overdrive.

I wanted to take control of this situation; so I was going to do my least favourite thing, just because I knew he would like it. I was going to give him a blow job, one he would never EVER forget. I moved down and down kissing every part of him, parting his legs and lying down on the floor on my front. Not taking my eyes off him, I took his penis in my mouth and began to suck.

DO IT RIGHT, NOT FAST! I kept repeating this in my head, I knew that I hated giving blow jobs from past experience, but I'd been taking a few notes from people about them recently. A few female friends had said that the first time you give a new man a 'great blow job', they will never forget you. I guess I didn't want him to forget me. Men have advised me that doing it slowly, taking your time and remembering to breathe is a good way forward. Nothing worse than a red-faced woman who looks like she's on speed on the end of your cock.

One person asked me if I liked ice cream, and I was confused by this concept. Apparently, if you can create a mental image of licking and eating your favourite ice cream, it's kind of similar to giving a good blow job, because an ice cream is enjoyable. Just don't get too carried away and stick a 99 right to the back of your throat practising, this would just look silly!

At first, I licked down the sides and round the tip, rolling my tongue and making it wet and easy to suck. Closing my eyes and imagining a Chocolate Feast, I nibble a little, trying hard not to take a bite out of it. I then sucked one of his balls, putting all of it in my mouth, the hair made me want to gag! Why don't men shave their balls too? Women don't like this; we shave, so should you!

Moving into a more comfortable position I put his entire fancy penis into my mouth, ALL of it, very, very slowly watching him, wanting to see what it did for him.

I repeated this slowly over and over again, making sounds as if I was enjoying it; it's like giving a fake orgasm – why do we make these sounds? I wasn't enjoying it very much, but I was enjoying watching him.

He looked at me with his big brown eyes as if to say, 'f*ck, what are you doing to me?' He tipped his head back in pure ecstasy; I must be doing a very good job. He loved this, and I did it for at least ten minutes before he pulled me off because he was about to cum, he then dragged me upstairs.

I had to pass the bathroom where I had done the giant fart, and chuckled to myself. His room was very messy, not like the rest of his house. He was weeks away from moving from his mansion to Buckingham Palace so he had stuff everywhere and I fell over a few things before getting to the bed.

He pulled me to the edge of the bed so my bottom was right on the edge and asked if I had ever had sex up the ass. I giggle loudly and said NO.

"So, do you want to try it?"

"I'm not really sure, is it going to hurt me? Will I need a medic?"

"Ha no, it's perfectly normal, loads of people do it."

"Well, do we need some sort of lubrication or something?"

"I have Vaseline."

"Well, OK, go get it then."

I started to shake; I was cold but I was absolutely terrified, what if something disgusting happened or worse, what if he broke my bottom and I had to go to hospital and explain how it happened? He returned with a tiny pot of Vaseline and smiled at me, but noticed I was shaking and asked if I was OK. I told him I was cold, and he reassured me that I wouldn't be for long. He got his fingers and poked me in my bottom with the lubrication on his fingers. I yelped – it hurt and I didn't much like it. He then told me to relax and started to enter me slowly. It wouldn't go in and I gave out a silly laugh and told him it wouldn't work. He did it again and he was in, f*ck it hurt so much! It reminded me of going to the loo the next day, after having had a strong vindaloo and too much to drink the night before.

He was very gentle and he was enjoying it so much I didn't have the heart to tell him it wasn't good for me. He finished and went to the bathroom to wash, and then came back and we made out for what seemed hours. All of it was amazing and felt really different, like I had just crossed a line of exploration and that I knew this man was going to teach me a lot. The worst thing going through my head was that this was the best sex I had ever had, meaning that either I have been shit in bed up until now or all of my previous partners had been.

The next morning, he walked me downstairs and gave me a kiss goodbye. I looked like a complete mess and even had to put my glasses on to drive home I like this man – he's quite cool. I can see me and his fancy penis meeting up on a regular basis, but God – he's given me a sore arse!

Chapter Eight
The Flasher

After taking my bottom virginity and turning me on like no one else ever has before, Fancy pants has yet again disappeared, so I have decided to keep my options open and go on a date.

After being on dating sites for a few months I have quickly learned so much about how to vet men!

I have compiled a list of questions I have to ask myself at appropriate parts of the evening, in order to understand my date and decide if I will take it any further. If I can do this beforehand, I simply will or will not see them, I have become quite brutal.

1. Do you or any of your family suffer from serious mental illness?

This rules out most of DSMI-V, having studied psychology I understand more than most, and recognise it quite quickly. I might avoid being murdered, raped or stalked if I can get this right first time!

2. If you have any slight detection of a wife or girlfriend lurking in the background, you will never EVER be successful with this man. Not only will he cheat on you, you could quite possibly be murdered by his psycho bitch.

A lot of these on-liners are out for a 'bit of cake and eat it'! Men think they are very good at hiding this, but forget that a wedding ring leaves a mark, and that

Facebook and Instagram are very accessible to the general public.

3. Do you have, or ever have had a tag? Seriously, there are some mad scary mother f*ckers out there that you need to protect your children AND yourself from. Ask about their CV and any gaps.

4. Addicts. Anyone who mentions they do drugs or get wasted off booze a lot, NOT a good idea. Rocky road to hell and back, been there before with someone, and I'm not going back again!

5. Time Wasters. People who waste your time, not ready to date and still not over their ex partners, or are too selfish because they have been on their own for so long that they have got used to themselves, and introducing someone new is exceptional and rare.

6. Over emotional, needy people. Total turn off – don't even bother! They will CRY on you, tell you for hours how they feel and you will never get a look in – they are on dating sites for free therapy and attention.

7. Sex. Plain and simple, just want a shag, no other motive. Players, damaged, angry, all of number 1.

8. Sick people. People who are actually dying, or fake an illness for you to feel sorry for them in order to try to get you to shag them. Yes, people DO stoop that low.

9. Predators! People who have been on dating sites for years, and wait for a NEW vulnerable, recently separated woman to join sites; one who looks desperate and needy – then they take FULL advantage of the situation.

10. The 1% you can't work out AT ALL, ones who give you no information and are completely guarded. AKA, 'Mr Fancy Pants.'
11. Men that say they are 'looking for the one', or being 'serious', or are just a 'nice guy who wants to find his other half'. It's ALL lies, they just say that because that is what you want to hear and they know it will attract women into thinking that they want a relationship.

Tonight, I had my first dinner date and he passed the entire test. We had been talking for weeks and he seemed to not fall into any of the aforementioned categories.

A lawyer, good job, good background, normal family, normal life – with a kind, attractive face, AND funny.

We met at a restaurant, very smart and formal. I wore a rather elegant dress and heels and no drinking beforehand so I was completely myself. I was a 'lady in red', turning up to have an intelligent conversation with a sexy lawyer who made me laugh and turned me on over texting.

I got to the restaurant and he sent me a text to say he was already at the table and to get the waiter to direct me. I followed his instructions and saw the face I recognized from the dating site, and, relieved that he was who he said he was, I started to walk to the table. The closer I got to the table the more I became aware that people were watching me and smirking. Jesus Christ Almighty, my date was, shall we say – vertically challenged; he was sitting on cushions to make him look taller in his chair. I shook his hand and sat down, feeling like my legs were not working due to shock, and didn't know what to do. It was not very PC of me to say, "Go f*ck yourself for not telling me the truth," but me being me I just got on with it. I suggested that we ordered wine and looked at the menu. I was not going to walk out on this poor man. He had actually been so kind to me for a few weeks texting; I should judge him on his height?

We ordered food and I drank my wine so quickly. I had to get pissed, trying to deal with the situation was hard. I must vet better next time, but remain kind at all costs. This is a test of my decency as a human being.

The food arrived and we started to eat, and I listened to his intelligent conversation about a court case he was 'not really allowed to talk about' which had taken place today. It was interesting and I soon forgot about his height, he was once more that funny intelligent man I'd been talking to on the phone.

Suddenly, out of nowhere, he became very forward, and started eating his food in a suggestive way. I laughed and drank more wine, feeling slightly awkward and talked about the fundamentals of friendship and how important it is to have that before anything else, to avoid it becoming serious or sexual. Guiltily I thought 'please can someone's dog die and phone me to get me out of this situation?'

Out of nowhere he held my hand and said he had a surprise for me. Innocently I did not expect or anticipate what followed. I thought he was going to offer to pay the bill! He looked into my eyes and I looked into his, he lead my hand under the table and put my hand on his rock hard dick. It was was bigger than he was – how the f*ck does THAT work?

I was sick in my mouth and so I made a swift excuse that I needed the toilet. After leaving my half of the bill with the waiter, and after washing my hands about twenty times, I exited via a fire escape. I lost a shoe in the process and ran faster than Forrest Gump to get a train home! I fell asleep on the train, because I'd drunk too much, and ended up at the train station, and got booted off. To my complete horror he was there, waiting for his train home and I had to hide from him. A pigeon shit on my dress and I missed my train. This resulted in me paying for a taxi which cost me the goddamn earth for a complete waste of my time.

New one to the list of vetting: 'Vertically Challenged Flashers' and double checking their height on profiles. F*CK!

Chapter Nine
Meow

Long day at work. God, travelling every day is killing me. I can't even do this job. I'm completely useless at being a boss. The only advantage of working for this company is the fact that the shops are local on my lunch break.

On my way home, after picking up the kids, my son completely embarrassed me in the petrol station doing his usual free thinking out loud, asking me why the fat man in the queue, was staring at my bottom. I grabbed the nearest bottle of wine and practically ran out of the shop. Came home to dog shit all over the place, a chewed bra and my best boots. I had evil thoughts about letting him out in the middle of the night so that he never came back again.

Homework, kids' uniforms, bath time, and bed.

I logged out of all the dating apps tonight. I had a date lined up now every free weekend for the next six weeks. I was talking to about twelve men, on an off, about their days, work and lives, getting completely confused especially after wine and calling everyone by the wrong names, getting everything mixed up. I don't have time for dating anyway; I'm far too busy pretending to be all important and successful. I'm lonely though and have to keep trying; if none of these men work out after having a date with them I will just see if I can let it happen naturally. Fancy pants is the unavailable invisible man, but I'm still hopeful.

I was just about to close my eyes when my phone rang and then hung up, and then pinged. Putting my glasses on I looked at my phone. Oh God, it had better not be work, I can't be bothered, I'm not interested and I'm so tired. It was 'Mr Fancy Pants'. My heart did a little panic puke and I was instantly smiling.

"Hey, how are you, cheeky? You free tonight?" Ah, 'Mr Fancy Pants' is still alive and well. I wonder if he's still going to be a massive fancy dick.

"Nope, too late to get a sitter too."

"Shame, oh well, your loss! You had any dick recently?"

"No! The last person was you. You know I'm not sleeping around. I have a few dates lined up though. You?"

"No, not had any dick either."

"Hahaha."

"So, you in bed?"

"Yeah."

"Show me your pussy!"

"I'm sorry, what?" It was direct but quite sexy. I was turned on but it was not how anyone else had been with me. I sent him a picture on WhatsApp of a bald Siamese cat, and text in capitals MEOW.

He didn't find it funny because he never replied and then he disappeared from WhatsApp. Moody much? I'm just having a bit of fun with him and I don't really know how to react to what he's just said to me; I've only slept with him twice.

Where the f*ck does he go? I'm sure it doesn't take that long to do most things. Is he talking to someone else because I'm not doing as I'm told or as he wants me to act with him? He disappears into a void of fanciness where I can't find him ALL the time.

I'd finished the bottle of red between typing up some notes from a meeting and him disappearing, and was now a little insecure about him going away.

Right! You want to be playful, 'Mr Fancy Pants F*cktard', I will show you playful!

I then sent him a WhatsApp recording of me naked and sexy on my bed. Immediately he came back. 'Mmmmm, am I going to get to see your pussy then?'

I sent him another WhatsApp video. 'Mr Fancy Pants, sit in an upright position and fasten your seat belt, you're in for a bumpy ride!' Giving him a cheeky little wink and scanning the phone over my naked body, teasing him and loving the control. 'So, Mr Fancy Pants, what do you want me to do next?'

'Get your toys out.'

I recorded another video. 'I don't know what you're talking about? What toys?' biting my lip and trying not to laugh. 'What are you thinking?'

'I'm thinking I want you to sit on your rabbit and film it.'

'Really? Are you serious? The poor thing might suffocate.'

'Hahaha.' Finally he finds something I say funny!

A little drunk and never having done this before I try my best to please him. What if it doesn't work or I break my vibrator? Placing the phone on my pillow and adjusting the screen so that it films my body, I get into position and press record. Looking at the image on the phone it has my full body kneeling down on the bed but not my face. I touch my breasts and run my hands down my body, down to my pussy and it feels wet already with the excitement. I start to play, and reach for the rabbit. Inserting the rabbit inside me I bear down and start a slow rhythm. To my delight it, felt amazing. How did I not know how to do this before? This is just like having sex with no man needed. I change the speed on the vibrator and start to moan, OMG this is so good. Thinking about him being there with me, I cum so hard and cry out his name, "Mr Fancyyyyy Pannnntssss!" The bed collapsed, throwing my phone onto the floor onto its front and sending the video without me watching it back first.

F*CK! He's going to piss himself laughing or think that I'm a total disaster. Frantically texting him, shaking from the shock of a massive orgasm and my bed collapsing, sending me flying at the same time.

'OMG. I'm so sorry, I have to go to fix my bed.'

No reply, off he fancy f*cks off again!

Wait a minute, why am I saying sorry? I've just been used!

Chapter Ten
Silhouette

Sick of watching Ben and Holly's magic fecking kingdom with the kids, the only magic wand I'm interested in has not bothered to contact me or to offer to help put my bed back together, after my amazing performance a few weeks ago. I think I've messed up, he must have seen something he didn't like and I don't think I will hear from him again.

I put the kids to bed and decided to actually watch a movie and stay in. After my horrific date, I'd put all the other men on hold for a bit; I didn't want any more shocks in public. *Train Spotting* was on the T.V. I love this movie, it's so real and so shocking, made me think that I should just love life and get addicted to what I love best, SEX!

After drinking a few glasses of wine, I started rambling on a bit, putting my take on the movie I stand up and recite. "Choose sex. Choose a blow job. Choose a divorce. Choose a f*cking big vibrator, a crap car, loud music and online dating. Choose wine, and high cholesterol. Choose your friends – be wise, DONT trust them all. Choose sexy underwear and hair extensions. Choose long hot baths and a range of smart priced bubbles. Choose having kids and wondering what the f*ck you are doing on a Sunday morning when you are at A&E because one of them has stuck a pea up the other one's nose for fun. Chose a dog that shits everywhere and chews all your underwear. Choose not paying your bills on time so you can go out and have more fun. Choose crazy naked dancing and singing at the top of your voice. Choose to be honest with yourself. Choose setting standards high. Choose what makes your feel happy! Choose laughter. Choose your future. Choose sex," (scientifically proven to put a smile on your face).

I was so bored, so I decided to text the reason I now sleep with a vibrator and broken bed.

'Good evening, you moved yet? You promised me a tour of your new house. Remember you said we were going to have sex in every room?'

'I've not moved, still in the old place, boxes everywhere.'

'Well do you need me to come help you 'unpack'?'

'I'm quite capable thank you.'

Oh God, he's not interested, just put myself out there and got rejected. I didn't respond.

'But I'd like to see you naked.' Panic over – he still finds me attractive. What the hell am I saying to myself, why should I be worried about this? I knew this anyway. What's going on in my head?

'Naked how/where?' I then got a picture of a silhouette of woman with her legs open, in heels, crouching down, her hips tilted forward.

'I want a picture of you doing this.'

I studied the picture for a few minutes, went to my room and took my clothes off. I stood in front of my mirror and tried to do the position, it was quite tricky but I managed it; now to try it in heels. You have never seen anything like it, I tried to do this in heels with my long legs, falling all over the place. I got cramp in my foot and my legs were shaking, I couldn't get a single picture right, it was taking ages.

'Where's my photo?'

'It's coming, stroppy fancy demanding walking hardon! This is harder than it looks!' This is not turning me on, why am I doing this for this man? I'm actually in pain to please him? 'You try getting naked and putting heels on and show me a picture of your hairy bottom and balls!'

After falling over several times I finally I got one decent picture of the position which he'd asked me to replicate. I then had to edit it and put filters on before sending it, to make it look better.

'Mmmmm that's hot, it's late, I'm tired. NIGHT!'

'What? I've just spent all that time putting all that effort into sending a picture of my most private parts and you are going?'

'I didn't make you, it was just a suggestion. Yeah, I'm tired.'

'It was only nine pm.' And he was gone.

I felt insecure but didn't want to say much more without seeming desperate. I went to bed worrying about what I'd just sent, what if he shows it to someone? I don't know him all that well. I know he seems to have his shit together, but I don't know what he's capable of. I sent a text asking him to delete the pic and he said he already had.

The next day I received a photo of him smiling at me from his car. My heart skipped a beat, he likes me. I'm falling, slowly, but I feel a massive tug of emotion towards him and we do have fun. I will just leave him be and let him come to me...

Chapter Eleven
The Naked Drive to 'Mr Fancy Pants'

I'm really starting to hate my job and the kids had driven me insane and I'm glad they have gone to their dad's house. All I wanted for my Friday night in was a glass of wine, a takeaway and a good f*ck. Checked my phone, one million messages from weirdos on POF that I'd become addicted to again through fancy pants ignoring me most of the time, a few emails and a WhatsApp.

I had the usual out of the blue text from 'Mr Fancy Pants': 'How's you?' which means I'm not really interested in your reply, but are you available to f*ck me tonight? I have actually deleted his number because he's pissed me off from the last time we spoke, so I ask who it is, play the 'I don't care' card. 'I didn't save your number.' Then we are quickly back into unemotional very naughty banter as if we had never left off.

"What are you doing right now?" Translates to: Take your clothes off and send me naked pictures so I can get in the mood. Even if it's not me he's going to shag, it's quite likely he's got someone else going round for a shag and needs the inspiration beforehand to get him horny. I swear he's had someone round just before me once, I could smell perfume. A production line of shags! I know this man and he thinks I'm stupid, it makes me want to smash his face in, but I'm afraid it's like giving up smoking, once you are addicted to it, it's hard to stop, and I'm addicted to his penis.

After a bit of back and forth chat, a dick pic and naked photo of me, we discuss what we are going to do with each other and how it's going to happen and most importantly, what I'm going to wear. He dared me to drive naked to his house. Challenge accepted!

I've driven half naked to his, wearing a coat before, sexy little dance and kitchen table flashback, but never completely naked. I felt so naughty, I couldn't wait to set off, but I did have in the back of my mind the possibility of my old clapped out car breaking down and having to call the AA. I arrive on time naked (with my coat on) on a very cold late December night, with very pert nipples! He opened the door to me, smiling widely.

It was the first time I had seen him in weeks and he had put on a few extra pounds, but still looked sexy. He doesn't know how to dress sometimes, though I never say anything but I do prefer him naked. I told him he looked nice as I always do (I'm very polite). He was obviously a little drunk, and had explained that he had been out all day – but could handle his booze and I was reassured he was 'good for sex'! Standing in high heels and a coat, I asked him if he was going to use his manners and take my coat off me. Off it came; I did a little spin around, a "TA-DAH" and laughed shouting, "Merry Christmas Mr Fancy Pants." Exposed and sexy, I felt amazing and free. How much fun was THIS? His face was a mixture of shock and lust. I don't think he expected me to follow the dare through. I kissed him, giggling, and we pressed up against each other; I felt him instantly hard.

To my surprise we headed to the kitchen instead of the bedroom and talked for a while. I sat on his kitchen counter completely naked for at least an hour talking about crap, and drinking. This was new, we are communicating. He's always been such a dick or told me to shut the f*ck up and thrown me on the bed/sofa/table/floor or stuck his penis in my mouth or slapped me with it.

Taking my drink off me he moved towards me and sucked my breasts while I was still sitting on the counter top. Pushing my legs open so he could get closer to kiss me I could hardly think, looking into his deep brown eyes, I whispered, "Finally."

Chasing me through the house and up the stairs giggling, he pushed me onto the bed and pulled my legs towards him, he had full control as always and I loved it. We had crazy, mad, passionate, every kind of naughty sex for hours. I even passed out a few times the sex was that good. I could do this with him all day every day forever. (Later I googled what happened with the passing out: it's called 'La petite mort'– little death, 'the brief loss or weakening of consciousness', and it refers to the sensation of orgasm as being likened to death). He nearly killed me, twice! I'd better get a defibrillator to leave at his house.

Weeks ago, I sent him a song that reminded me of us, we don't date, we have never been out anywhere, we just meet up for sex at his when HE wants it. I send him texts, he reads them and never replies. I can have full blown conversations with myself to him and never get a response, like a crazy person, especially after wine when I'm at my worst, the poor man gets it all. On one of these occasions, I had sent him a text on WhatsApp with a song attached called 'Starving', saying that it reminded me of our sex.

I was on top riding him when 'Starving' came on his play list. He looked at me with his sexy little smile and gasped in surprise that it had come on. I covered my face with my hands, how embarrassing. He had remembered, but he had never replied to my message when I sent him the song. He does read my messages AND pays attention. I'm in shock. Who is this person I am seeing for the first time tonight and what's he done with 'Mr 'always a bastard' Fancy Pants'?

We carried on making out for a bit longer and then alcohol took over and then both of us were useless in bed. I stayed over, and lying in bed facing each other, he asked me a question. "What does all this mean to you?" I couldn't believe he asked me that, are you serious, what the hell is this?

I was not prepared for this emotional level of conversation and I was now drunk, and although I knew that my feelings were starting to get complicated with him and confusing, I didn't know the answer. I wasn't ready to say 'love', so I simply said, "I don't know." I asked him the same question, and he gave me the same answer, we both looked up to the ceiling and didn't speak.

I'm not in love with this man? He's older and he has shit slippers! I don't like his taste in clothes and he's a first class dickhead! He might have a fancy house, car and job, but that's not important to me. I like his penis, it's his penis I'm in love with not him. Isn't it? F*ck! I really don't know.

The sleepover was entertainment in itself. He stank of garlic and snored his head off all night and worst of all he kept farting! I didn't get much sleep, and wanted to suffocate him with his pillow and shove something up his bottom. Payback for doing it to me.

I kissed his fancy penis goodbye and I let myself out in the morning. Driving home naked and with carpet burns was a cold and uncomfortable experience. But something had changed. What the hell am I going to do? I have a date tonight - why do I feel guilty? I text him to let him know I was home safely, and guess what? READ and IGNORED! I could think of a few choice words.

Chapter Twelve
Mr Millionaire Strawberry Psycho

'Mr Fancy Pants' still doesn't make time for me so I get on with my life and continue to go on dates. I've ended up back on dating sites because I'm not meeting people on nights out with the girls. Seem to be constantly off and on.

I think it's my age; no one seems to look at me, and if they do they are overweight or old and ugly. If I do get approached I like to talk to them and find out about them, but they usually get bored and walk away, or make an excuse, or go to the bathroom; men literally run away. My friends actually got the DJ in the bar we were at to play 'Another one bites the dust' to take the fun out of me for managing to scare off three men in one night, my record so far.

I'm being very brave and going on a date with a semi famous footballer tonight. He's doing the cooking and I'm taking the wine and desert. He lives in a mansion house and is a millionaire, or so he says.

We have talked on the phone all day every day for a week, constantly texting and get on so well I am quite looking forward to the date and the possibility of a little kiss at the end of the night. I feel as excited as I have done with 'Mr Fancy Pants' but this one shows me a lot more attention and seems to want to continue this as a relationship, long term.

I was getting into my dress when I got a text on my phone and then a missed call, running across the room half dressed to see what 'Mr Millionaire' wanted, but to my surprise it was 'Mr Fancy Pants'.

"Hey, how's you?"

"You do pick your timing; I'm just about to go out."

"Who's the lucky man tonight then?"

"A famous footballer actually, he's a millionaire." I sent him a WhatsApp of the mansion house I'd be driving to tonight and all its grounds.

"Pretty cool right? Never dated a celeb before, and he's cooking so it's a real date."

"Yeah, be good to knock around with money I suppose. Bet he doesn't have a dick as good as mine though."

"Well, have a look for yourself, I will let you work that one out." I proceeded to send 'Mr Jealous Fancy Pants' a picture of the footballer's dick in all its glory, just to prove a point to him that I can get laid if I want to, with someone who is amazing and that I didn't need his fancy dick. Put that in your fancy pipe and smoke it! I'm giving him some attitude back, two can play at this game.

"Look, I have to go, I'm going to be late. Bye."

"Well that's a decent size, you will have fun with that, have a good time."

That hurt, oh my God he's good at this, he always has the last word. Yes I do only want you, you stupid man, but you won't give yourself to me and I'm not waiting until I'm old and grey to stick around waiting for you to make your mind up.

"Who said I'm going to, it's a first date!"

"Didn't stop you with me."

"That was different."

"Yeah yeah."

"Look, it's just a dinner. You've ignored me for the last two weeks, I do have a life you know. You just wanted to be friends, right?"

"I never said that."

"What? It's what you implied, nothing serious. You never say anything, so what am I supposed to think? I'm late, I have to go. Bye." I was in such a good mood thinking that I was going on an exciting adventure tonight, now all I can think about is 'Mr Put A Massive Downer On My Night W*nker Pants'.

All the way to 'Mr Millionaire's house I couldn't stop thinking about the possibility that I might have upset him or missed out on an opportunity to be with him again. I nearly turned around and set off to his house just to kiss him and tell him I was sorry, but then raised a question in my head that I might not have been the first call tonight. He will probably have already gone out or found someone else to shag; not sure I could stand to see him with anyone else.

I had brought some tiramisu, a few bottles of red wine and some strawberries for the date. I made sure I'd not eaten all day so I didn't waste any of his food. He said he was a good cook so I was really looking forward to it. Using the sat nav I arrived at his gates and didn't get lost, the driveway was long and the grounds were beautiful. He had a water fountain at the front of the house that I nearly hit, trying to park my crap rusty car in his oh so very posh driveway.

I sat in the car for a few minutes to gather myself, because I was nervous. I looked on WhatsApp at 'Mr

Fancy Pants' picture and thought to myself, if you'd just pulled your finger out of your asshole and asked me out, I'd not have to go through any of this.

I gracefully got out of the car and he was already standing at the door waiting for me. He looked very handsome and had a warm welcoming smile; everything was going to be OK. He took the food and wine off me and gave me a kiss on each side of my face, a complete gent.

As we walked though his house I think my jaw must have been on the floor. Marble everywhere, expensive elaborate furniture, it was like nothing I had ever seen or been in before. When I realised he had a pool, I gave a little yelp.

I felt uncomfortable, not because of the fact that he had so much money, but the fact that it didn't feel like a home. It was all show, it wasn't cozy or relaxed. My house had clutter and crap cushions and my personality all over it, this was clinical and cold and unloved. I think a house can reflect a personality and he was sad and lonely I could tell, no love lived here.

I needed wine, and we had already discussed that he had five bedrooms and I could pick any one to sleep in tonight so I intended to get a bit tipsy. He cooked and we talked and drank wine, we got on like a house on fire. I was really enjoying my evening. I got a bit closer to him by kicking my shoes off and sat on the counter next to him, watching him chop up an onion. My legs were dangling over the edge of the unit; he then grabbed one of my feet and put it on the counter top, I smiled as I thought he was going to give me a foot rub or kiss my foot. To my horror he got the knife he had been cutting onions with and held it over my toes, he put it to my skin so I could feel the cold edge of the knife and he looked into to my eyes grinning. I couldn't even pull away or he would have cut me, I just looked at him and asked him what the f*ck he was doing and gave out a nervous laugh. My heart was pounding; Jesus, I'd gone on a date with Dexter to a house in the middle of nowhere, and I was his next murder victim. He pulled the knife away and laughed at me, then grabbed me and kissed me. I dare not kiss him back – he still had the knife in his hand.

There was something wrong with this man and I was not going to get away easily. I'd already watched him lock the door and put the alarm on when I arrived, I didn't even think. He said he had security issues, and cameras everywhere, and I believed him.

I made an excuse to go to the bathroom, locked the door and threw up in the toilet. I reached in my bag and got my phone out. There was no signal because this house was in the middle of nowhere and no way could I call anyone for help. I started to cry. If only I'd gone to 'Mr Fancy Pant's house instead, I might see tomorrow. I need to be smart and stay one step ahead of him all night and try to get him very drunk so I could escape. I walked back into the kitchen and dinner was on the table with candles and more wine. I looked nervously at him and sat down saying, "Thank you."

He asked what was wrong and I said I was not feeling very well and that maybe I should go home. He told me to eat and that I couldn't drive after all the wine I'd drunk and that he would run me a nice hot bath and I could get some sleep after the meal.

Over dinner he started to talk about sex and asked me when was the last time I'd had any. Alarm bells were ringing in my head, there is no way on God's earth I would be having sex with this man. All the texts before that I had sent him were because I thought he was normal, how wrong could I have been? We had dinner and he washed up, everything had to be spotless and in its place. It unnerved me so much. I drank some wine and said a bath would be nice, (at least I could escape and lock myself in the bathroom until I could come up with a plan).

We walked the full length of the house and arrived at a massive master bedroom with a big four-poster white bed. It looked out over the land where my dead body could possibly be buried, and no one would ever find me; for the first time a beautiful landscape terrified me. The bathroom was as big as his kitchen and it had an old traditional bath, like on the Flake adverts; it looked very inviting. Two massive candlesticks were on the windowsill, but the candles had never been lit. This room didn't get used a lot. There were no towels, no soap, no toilet roll. Was this even his house? Was he just looking after it for someone? Was I going to die tonight without ever getting the opportunity to see 'Mr Fancy Pants Please Come And Save Me' again?

He turned the bath taps on and said he was going to get some towels. Perfect opportunity! I immediately said I was going for a wee and shut the door, reaching for the lock, but it didn't have one. F*ck, I sat on the toilet having a wee, rocking, with my arms around me like a mental person, trying not to cry. He knocked on the door and came in while I was still pulling my pants up. He was completely naked and was carrying strawberries in bowls, some more wine and a small knife. I froze and he turned to me and started to undress me, grabbing the back of my head and kissing me aggressively and I could feel him getting hard. I was in no position to argue or push him away with a knife in the bathroom and no idea what he was capable of doing to me. I went along with whatever sordid idea he had for this night and kept calm. I didn't want to die.

We both got in the bath and he started to relax and talked about his ex-partner for what seemed forever. He got quite upset and started to cry, telling me how much he loved her and how much I reminded him of her. He reached for the strawberries and the knife and started cutting them up in the bowl, so I kept still and watched his every move.

Eating them, he finally put the knife down and asked why I wasn't eating mine, I said I wasn't hungry. Laying there in the bath, with a psychopath, how the f*ck did this happen to me, of course I wasn't hungry.

"So, what are your fantasies?"

"What do you mean?"

"What turns you on most of all?"

"Lots of things."

"What would you like to do to me right now?"

I could think of a few things: stab him with the knife and run as fast as I could, put his head under the water, and kick him in the balls maybe? I had to think fast and smart. "I'd like to tie you to the bed, and blindfold you and then f*ck you stupid."

"Would you eat those strawberries off my dick? I will let you do that if you eat them off me."

I paused and thought to myself, it's probably going to put me off them for the rest of my life but I'm going to have to do this in order to escape. I nodded in agreement and he started to play with me in the water, so I suggested we got out. We got out of the bath and he dried me, holding my hand behind my back he walked behind me, guiding me to the bedroom. He pushed me onto the bed face down and then flipped me over and kissed me so hard my lips started to hurt. I pushed him off me and onto his back, trying to take control of the situation, pretending I was really turned on.

The strawberries were at the side of the bed; he grabbed the bowl and tipped them all over his penis, then pushed my head down. I started to eat them wanting to be sick, every mouthful seemed to take so long and he was really enjoying getting off on this. I stopped and said, "What am I going to tie you up with then?" trying to play the game, looking interested and sexy.

He reached into a drawer by his bed and pulled out a few ties, and threw them at me. I grabbed the psycho's hand and pulled it to the bedpost, securing it as tightly as I could, not caring if I hurt him. I repeated this with his other hand and then blindfolded him with another tie.

"Are you going to f*ck me now you sexy baby girl?"

"In your f*cking dreams you psychopathic freak! You really think I don't know what you are trying to do to me? I'm off and I hope no one ever f*cking finds you!"

He jolted up in bed, pulling at the ties, and I was again terrified. I ran as fast as I could, not even stopping to get dressed. I grabbed my bag and car keys but left my clothes and shoes. I ran down the driveway naked and got in my car. I was covered in sticky strawberry juice, but that didn't matter. The house alarm was making so much noise, it would definitely raise the alarm to the police.

I had had far too much to drink to be driving so I called the police and explained that I had had to drive half a mile to a safe place and hide, and that I was naked and I needed someone to come and collect me, to take me home. It didn't take long for the police to arrive. I opened the car door to the officer, naked and covered in strawberry juice, crying and shaking. He went to his car and came back with a blanket, put me in his car and took me to the station to give a statement. All the way there we were in complete silence other than, "You'll be OK, love, let's get you a nice warm drink."

Chapter Thirteen
I Don't Give a Flying F*ck

I was dressed in a sexy air hostess outfit, fishnet stockings and a push-up bra – I am ready for my captain. Pushing the trolley down the length of the plane, drinking a small bottle of wine in one go, shouting to the people on the plane, "Free wine and beer, please help yourself," the Top Gun theme tune was playing at full blast, and I was doing a few little twirls and sexy dancing all the way down the aisle.

I got a cheeky slap on the bottom and a thank you, I winked and carried on walking, getting closer to the cockpit. The people on the plane were going wild so I turned to them and asked them to start clapping as I opened the cockpit door, shouting to everyone, "Wish me luck," I got a massive round of applause and whistling.

'Mr Sexy F*cker Pilot Pants' was sitting in his seat flying the plane. I could see the side of his expressionless face in total concentration. His sexy slightly grey sideburns and his beautiful neckline and a captain's hat were all he was wearing.

"Is there anything I can get you, captain? Drink?"

"Well that depends on the hostess, and how wet she is."

I rolled down my slightly moist knickers and turned his chair round to face me, took them off and put them to his nose and let him feel them on his lips. "Wet enough for you?"

"No – we need to do something about that don't we?" He looked me in the eyes and reached for his microphone. "This is your captain speaking. We have reached thirty thousand feet and hit some turbulence, please fasten your seat belts until further notice." He pressed cruise control and spoke to the control room, then turned to me, got up and walked around me tapping his fingers on his lips.

"What are you going to do to me, captain?" I gave out a little giggle and touched his beautiful lips with my finger, still wet from taking my pants off.

"Shut the f*ck up and bend over," and with a little smirk, he pushed me onto the front of the plane, face forward so I could look out into the clouds. He started to lick me, sticking his tongue right inside and then his fingers and then both, alternately. I was moaning and getting so wet, the clouds were making me dizzy and I screamed out for him to stop. "Miss hostess, you work for me. You do as you're f*cking told!"

"Yes, captain, whatever you say."

"Turn round."

"How do you want me?"

My high heels were causing me a problem, making me slide off the controls, so he took them off and threw them on the floor. He took his hat off and put it on me, his steady hands making their way down my body. Watching my every move, he then ripped my uniform blouse open, exposing my bra. He grabbed my breasts and squeezed them hard, then gave one hard tug and my uniform was off. I could hardly control my body, my heart was pounding with excitement but I remained confidant yet submissive and let him take command. He grabbed my chin and kissed me, his brown eyes burning into mine. He then slowly pushed himself inside me. He held my bottom while he thrust hard inside me, again and again and again. He had never been this rough before; he f*cked me hard, so hard my hat fell off.

"If you're going to squirt, don't do it on my control panel or we will all die."

"OK, get me off here – I'm getting close."

He picked me up and walked to the cockpit door, opened it completely naked and we both got a massive round of applause. He did a little bow and got me to do one too. Both of us were giggling, he then picked me up and pushed my back against the cabin door, which was not very wide. My legs were too long to fit, so he bent my knees so my feet were pushing against the wall and lowered me to the level in line with his fancy cock, and we were on show and about to f*ck again.

With everyone watching, applauding and shouting encouragement he f*cked me hard in front of them all, smiling at me and biting his lip as if he had the devil in him. My head banging against the door, it didn't last long but we both came at the same time, and when he lowered me down I could feel how hard he still was inside me. My legs shaking, we re-entered the cockpit and he shut the door. He pushed me against the wall and began kissing me, pinning me to the wall and starting all over again. We were broken off by the control room on the radio. "Goose, you big STUD, get back to flying the f*cking plane, will you?"

"Roger that," and he was back in his seat, fully dressed with his sexy hat on. God Almighty, I could just sit here and watch him forever.

I opened the cabin door naked and started walking down the aisle; it was like no one had ever seen me before and they were disgusted by the fact that I was completely naked, gasping and covering their eyes. I turned around and a giant strawberry was behind me wearing a captain's hat. I started to run but couldn't get anywhere, it was like running on a treadmill. I looked all around me and everyone in their seats had now turned to strawberries. Strawberries were coming from everywhere and smothered me. I could smell them and feel them all wet and sticky.

I woke up, OMG. It's me who's wet and sticky, girls can have wet dreams?

Chapter Fourteen
Help Me Obi Wan Kenobi

Since the incident with the psychopath, I've had a few weeks of reflection and stayed away from anything to do with dating or talking to men. The police said that he was unknown to them, but they would keep an eye on the situation and had a very direct conversation with me about 'stranger danger'.

The only person that drifted into my thoughts, no matter how hard I tried for him not to was 'Mr Fancy Pants Doesn't Deserve My Time, Fit As F*ck Wish He Would Call Me Pants'. My finger held over his name to call him, then I thought twice – he never answers anyway and he probably had his head buried somewhere between another girl's legs.

I looked through my phone book and decided to call 'Mr Star Wars'. He answered the call, surprised. "Hello, you."

"Hey, how are you? I'm sorry to call so late, are you free to talk? I kind of need some advice."

"Sure, is it a bottle of wine conversation or a quick five minutes?"

"It's a few bottles of wine conversation a silver bullet and a gun. I'm quite confused. I think I might have fallen in love with someone more complicated than me, with someone who doesn't love me back."

There was a long pause and a deep sigh. "You have my full attention, young lady. Get a bottle of wine cracked open and let's push on until the early hours. Right, OK. This is serious then?"

"Yeah you could say that. My head's obsessing, I'm waking up thinking about this man, dream about him when I go to bed at night and waking up still thinking about him. This has never happened before and I can't shake it off. It's not just that, I'm having full blown conversations with myself over text messages. He just reads them and ignores me, and so I think he's listening to me and I write more, making it worse and then having to say sorry all the time. I literally feel like I'm going insane."

"Does he feel the same about you?"

"I can't work it out; he seems to want me when I am with him but the rest of the time, it's limited conversation. When he's nice, he's really amazing, when he's detached or distant from me, it's pretty harsh and horrible."

"Well, what's happening? I'm confused."

"You remember that date I had? I gave you an address so you knew where I was? Well, it's still him. We randomly meet up for sex, but it's never me who says when, he just calls me up and I go to his house and I can't stop going, it's like I'm addicted."

"So, you are f*ck buddies, a booty call?"

"I consent to it, I love it, it's so exciting when I am with him. I actually can't wait for the next time, the sex is unbelievable and we have such a good laugh too."

"So, what's the problem?"

"Feelings have started, like I say, I'm obsessing and weird shit."

"You want him to be your boyfriend?"

"This is the strangest thing. No, I'm not ready for that yet, but I want him to stop ignoring me and be consistent. Pay me respect, admit that he has some sort of feelings for me. When he ignores me, I feel like I'm actually going mad, I hate not knowing what he's thinking."

"Hang on a minute, he ignores you?"

"Yes, we talk before sex, then have sex and then he talks to me for a bit more, then just disappears. He's like a ghost, a ghost who reads my messages. I can see that he does actually read them. It really upsets me and I have no idea what's going on."

"That's really rude; it's out of order to treat someone that way. It only take a few seconds to text back and say you're busy or can't talk."

"I know. I don't think I'd ever do that to anyone. If I've had to answer back because I didn't want to talk to them I would explain why, not leave them guessing, it's a horrid thing to do, right? He keeps me guessing ALL the time, I have no idea what he's thinking or feeling. This makes me want him more, and that's just insane."

"Babes, he doesn't care about you, sorry I know it's harsh but he really isn't interested."

"What, really? He doesn't? I mean I thought it but actually hearing someone saying it is different. So why does he keep contacting me if he doesn't like me?"

"Because he wants to f*ck you; you must be good if he's not bored of you after all this time, with no commitment. You are just a f*ck to him, nothing more. Does he turn on the charm before you meet up to make you think you are special?"

"Yeah. I don't know where he starts and where I end – it's all consuming, like magic. When I'm with him it's been the best moments of my sex life, no comparison to anyone."

"Oh cheers!"

"Don't be like that. You know I love you, but we are just mates."

"I know babes I was joking, but seriously, you're not in love, you're in lust."

"I've never felt like this before about anyone. I don't know what this is, do I tell him? We have just been really silly up until now, just naughty with each other but it's been months. Surely, if I feel something so strongly, should I tell him?"

'Mr Star Wars' gave out a laugh of amusement. "He won't want to hear it! He won't want what you want I'm certain of it. But hey, I don't know why the guy should act like a massive dickhead though if I'm honest, you can do so much better. When have you not been able to express your feelings? Come on, you're the most emotional 'say it how it is' person I have ever met. You wear your heart on your sleeve and everyone knows how loving you are, it's one of the best things about you, but also you're your own worst enemy!"

"Well I'm ready to give up looking and just be with him. I've deleted all the dating sites and stopped talking to other men. I'm ready to exclusively be his buddy until further notice, so I guess I'll just give him all my time until he says it's game over, or he hurts me and I realise he is a dick and let him go."

"Wow, I thought you were having loads of fun? You must have been on what, forty dates by now?"

"Yeah, about that, but if I have to sit through one more movie, drink another coffee or listen to someone over dinner I might go commit suicide. I'm bored shitless and all I ever think about when I'm with other people is what I could be doing if he was with me, so is it not a pointless waste of time and money?"

"Young lady, you have got it bad. I don't know what to suggest. Go out and shag someone else?"

"I have tried that, twice, and kicked him out; it felt like I was cheating on him so didn't go any further with it."

"Yep, you're f*cked. You actually might be starting to fall in love, but if you are, you need to snap out of it because the behaviour he is displaying is not love, he doesn't feel the same. How long since you've been in contact?"

"Almost three weeks. We have never been out on one date in six months."

"A once a month shag, he has a girlfriend. Does he call you when it's her time of the month?"

I went deadly silent; oh God, does he have a girlfriend? I've never seen anything at his house to indicate that a female might live there or be part of his life though. I've been in all his rooms apart from the kids' rooms, no – this can't be true.

I walked to the fridge and pulled out some tiramisu and a bottle of wine and continued to listen to him. I felt completely shit, useless and pointless and most of all really stupid. "I'm so lonely; I'm going to be alone forever aren't I?"

"Look, I felt like that when I split from my wife, but I have the kids and friends and you. Sure it would be nice to cuddle up with someone and have that closeness but it takes time, you've only been single a very short time, don't push it so much, just let it happen."

"But I put so much effort into everything, and I'm NOT afraid to express myself in anyway shape or form, I'm rare."

"You can be a bit scary too if I'm honest, it can be overwhelming that you try so hard. Just relax or I will have to come over to yours and kick you in the fanny! You are HOT, and bright and fun and lovely. Have you ever thought you might be intimidating to a man?"

"No, not ever. You know I don't think of myself as anything special, I just like to be real. I can't help but be real."

"I think you need to put this into perspective, and I know you won't listen to me and just do your own thing because you always do, but you are a catch, any man is very lucky to even get close to you. I loved our time together, but I'm glad we are good friends and would never want that to change, but you did scare me at first, wanting to change your Facebook profile to 'in a relationship' after a week – that's scary shit!"

"Oh God, I just got carried away with you, my Obi Wan Kenobi. A long time in a galaxy far, far away, I'd been waiting for you, Obi Wan! The circle is now complete, ha!"

"Remember, the force will be with you, always!"

"Yes, the force is strong with this one."

"Judge me by my size, do you? Fear is the path to the dark side."

"Attachment is forbidden. Unconditional love and answers calls to me every day about my dickhead f*ck buddy is essential to a Jedi's life!"

"Be mindful of your thoughts, Miss Wannabe Fancy Pants, they'll betray you! I sense great fear in you, Miss

Fannyfart, you have hate. You have anger. Smack him in the face?"

"Thanks for bringing that up. Good roleplay, banter over!"

"Shut up and go put your Princess Leia outfit on for me, you know how much I love it."

I sent him a picture of me in my Princess Leia gold bikini, accompanied by the words "Help me, Obi Wan Kenobi, you're my only hope!"

Not able to stop laughing, we both say goodnight and I hang up, still feeling completely confused.

Chapter Fifteen
The Doctor

A mental disorder, also called mental illness or psychiatric disorder, is a behavioural or mental pattern that causes significant distress or impairment of personal functioning. I had to see a doctor, not only could I not sleep or eat, I was starting to daydream and not be able to do my job properly. I was getting so tired and agitated and drinking a few bottles of wine a week to cope with the rejection from 'Mr Fancy Sending Me Mental Cheers A Million Pants'.

I wasn't going to message him, and he clearly wasn't going to message me; we had reached a stalemate. I guess the fun was over and he had found some other poor victim to mess around. Four weeks was a long time to not text someone you'd been intimate with, wasn't it? Especially when it was all relatively new.

I went to the surgery and opened the door to find a male doctor sitting in the chair, rather dashing- looking and full of smiles. "Good morning, please sit down. How can I help you today?"

"Well, it's kind of complicated and a little bit embarrassing. I've come about two things really."

"OK, just take your time."

"I've been having an 'open relationship' for the last six months. He's been sleeping with other people (I think), and I have too. I have used protection but don't know if he has and when we are together we don't use anything. I have foolishly trusted him and now we have lost contact. If I was to approach him to ask him the question I think he might get extremely offended, so I guess I'm just looking after myself.

"An open relationship…"

"Yes, 'f*ck buddies'. Are you familiar with the term? It's new age dating for the over 30s, I'm afraid."

"Right, OK then." He coughed awkwardly and did lots of typing. "So, you need testing for STDs?"

"Well, I think it's best to, don't you?"

"Yes, absolutely. Do you need condoms? We can supply them for you."

"No thank you, I have lots of them at home." I blushed and so did he.

"So, I can give you a test kit to take to the toilet. You just insert it into your vagina and take a swab and bring it back to me; would you like to do it now? The results should come back in a week."

"Yes, I can do that now." I blushed scarlet, his posh voice saying vagina turned me on.

"Do you want to be tested for Aids too? It's very rare but best to get it checked. I wouldn't be doing my job properly unless I informed you of this. It's more common with anal sex, so you should be fine."

I looked at him with a very worried expression. I didn't need to speak to explain what it meant and why I needed to take the test.

"Right. I will book you in for that too." He cleared his throat and the redness in his face deepened. He explained that I would have to have a blood test and then another, repeated in three months' time. I nodded in agreement and the appointments were arranged.

"And the other thing you came about?" He turned to me, now the redness had gone and he looked cool, calm and collected.

"I think I might be mentally ill."

He looked shocked, turned to his computer screen, looked at my notes, and then turned back. "Can you describe your symptoms to me?" He looked serious now, and in deep concentration.

"I have become obsessed with sex, and I'm unable to control myself. I have thoughts popping into my head about penises a few times a day at least. This is not about sex with lots of people though, it's just one man. I am forming a very unhealthy obsession with this man. I can't help but text him or try to get his attention. I actually talk to myself by text, have full blown conversations with no reply from him, but continue to text anyway. That's not normal, surely? Don't people with schizophrenia do stuff like this? I daydream about him and can't do my work properly, I can't eat or sleep. I have a massive sense of euphoria when I'm in contact with him, then low and depressed when I'm not. I feel like I'm on a roller-coaster, in between heaven and hell."

"Ah, it's nothing to worry about at all. This is described most commonly as either infatuation, love or lust." He gave me an unbelievable big smile, and I blushed.

"Well, is there a pill for it?"

"I'm afraid not, there is only time." He gave me a comforting smile.

"What about hypnosis? People get cured of addictions like smoking, don't they? I'm sure that someone could put a mental image in my mind to not putting things I shouldn't in my mouth – it's the same as a cigarette."

The doctor looked at me with complete shock. "Well, no one's ever put that to me before, but I can ask for you."

"I just want this to go away, you do understand don't you? I have never been out of control like this. No one has ever affected me so that my behaviour completely changes. I know I am responsible for my own actions, but I'm really struggling here, so anything you can do to help would be great."

I got the usual show of leaflets about healthy diet and fitness. I thanked the doctor for his help, left with a handbag full of condoms anyway and a pee stick. As I was leaving he said, "Here is my personal mobile number. If you need ANYTHING at all, day or night, please doesn't hesitate to contact me. I don't live far from you and I'm just a phone call away." His eyes had a wicked gleam in them and my stomach lurched.

Oh my God, the hot doctor is hitting on me! I was actually quite flattered; he was intelligent and a DOCTOR after all, perhaps I will call him and he can be the second person whose willy I practice putting a bandage on.

Chapter Sixteen
Bubbadick

It's getting beyond a joke, I mean come on, seriously? Why do men on dating sites insist that by showing me a picture of their penis, I'm somehow going to want to magically message them back and have a whirlwind love affair? Dangle your silly little sausages somewhere else, you stupid perverts.

Doesn't make much difference anyway; the only one-eyed monster I want to see is 'Mr Fancy Pants', who can't be bothered to call me, pissing in the wind even trying to be with him. Beautiful, amazing, perfect fancy penis.

I've seen fat ones, small ones, I can't really see it ones, old ones, massive ones, ones with spots on, ones that haven't been washed, ones that look like aliens, leaking ones, exploding ones, that's NOT really yours ones, pretty pink ones, one eye close up evil ones, hairy ones, shaved ones, smart ones, tidy ones, possible STD ones, a little bit green ones, floppy ones, tired ones, overused ones, porn star ones, hello I'm peeking through my boxers ones, I can see your bum too ones, cold ones, shy ones, grey pubic hair ones, ones with one ball, ones with bigger balls than their penis, ones covered in chocolate, ones covered in cream, ones wearing accessories, ones in action, ones standing to ATTENTION, triumphant ones, ones inside someone's, but mostly boring 'oh it's another one'.

I could message half of Facebook and tell your wives and girlfriends about your silly little willies...LEAVE ME ALONE! Karma, all of your efforts will fail, you will continue to have shit sex, you will most likely catch STDs or worse AND I AM NOT GOING TO F*CK YOU.

I will just have a quick look at number twenty-three before I delete them all.

I've even started putting filters and funny faces on them to make them more interesting. It's getting old now, last head count (no pun intended) sixty-four strange monsters from the lagoon.

Chapter Seventeen
Cowboy Boots and Mirrors!

I came back from work today knowing that there was something seriously wrong with the finances of the company. We are not making money and I've not been there long. Going back to work for the company was such a good confidence boost for me. The last time I'd worked for them I managed to buy my own house and be completely self-sufficient. I was hoping that history was going to repeat itself and my life was going to get back on track after taking a financial hit by leaving my husband.

The word 'broke' is even in my street name, how ironic. I have a crap town house that I rent not far from the children's school, have hardly any furniture and what furniture I do have had been chewed or pissed on by the dog. I hate the fact that I can't afford to get out of this continuing financial struggle of being paid and then paying out for childcare and having virtually nothing left. If I lost my job my big shot attitude about being able to do everything for myself without my husband would go out of the window, and I would need help. I don't want help, and I won't take it.

I put the children to bed and watched them sleeping for a few minutes. There is nothing more beautiful in the world than seeing your children asleep, not able to answer you back or fight with each other. Just a perfect image of innocence and peacefulness. I loved them both so much and am so scared of not doing my best by them; but I was feeling worried and stressed about the future.

I decided I needed to try to relax so I lit some candles in the bathroom and got into a very hot bubble bath, with a bottle of wine. F*ck it, it was early and I needed to get this bottle down me tonight, no work tomorrow and I'm feeling like everything's out of my control; this had to help me forget.

I had a bit of confidence after drinking a glass of wine and I decided to just take a chance and text 'Mr Fallen Off The Face Of The Earth Fancy Pants'. Worst case: I don't get a reply or I'm blocked. I sent a picture on WhatsApp of my feet by the candles on the bath edge, with a glass of wine emoji and a devil's face. I sat back in the bath and left the phone on the side.

PING.

'Don't burn your toes!'

My heart skipped a beat; he's still around and texting back – quickly too. A massive smile spread across my face and I began to text back, trying not to drop my phone in the bath. 'Where have you been? You haven't texted or called.'

'Work work work, been all over the county.'

'Oh, well I've missed you.' He sent a blushing emoji and I sent one back.

'So, are you playing?' Here we go, God that didn't take long did it?

'In the bath? Really. I don't think the sensation would be very good in the tub.'

'Why don't you get out and go into the bedroom then?'

'You in a naughty mood?'

'Yeah, are you?'

'When am I not?' I then thought to myself, I haven't been for a while, not without my inspiration to do anything, maybe it's a bit of stress or maybe it's just him? I got out of the bath, grabbed my bottle of wine and headed upstairs. I laid down on my bed and sent him a video recording of me on the bed, saying that he had my full attention.

'Do you have any new toys or same old faithfuls?'

'I have all new ones actually. I bought a few things I thought you might be excited by but then never heard from you.'

'Haha, you have? What? Show me!'

I grabbed a box from underneath my bed and tipped it out. It was a selection of whips, chains, blindfolds and vibrators. One of them was very expensive – 'the lush vibrator' – it could be controlled by an iPhone app and you could activate it from anywhere in the world. It is voice controlled, and you can set it to music and let yourself fall to the mercy of your partner, or better still, you can wear it everywhere you go.

I sent him a picture on WhatsApp with a brief description of what they did and ranked them in order of most exciting by using a star emoji. I then recorded another video of me whipping myself between my legs, thinking to myself, this will send him wild. After a few minutes with no reply I became concerned, was he put off by it?

'What's wrong, did you not like?'

'It's not naughty enough.' How rude! I was really turned on doing that. He's still such a bastard.

'Oh, gosh. Right then… errrmm.'

'F*ck yourself with your rabbit vibrator, on all fours, I want to see you cum.'

I sent him a photo of me kneeling down with my vibrator positioned toward the entrance of my pussy, and attached the theme tune from Jaws. I was a little drunk and always knew how to kill the mood by my silly sense of humour.

Silence again.

'Oh come on, that was funny!' I was laughing my head off so much I got the hiccups.

'Yes, it made me chuckle.'

I then sent him another recording of me slowly inserting the vibrator inside me, and saying, "I want you now, and I want you to cum inside me."

'I will cum where the f*ck I like!'

Oh my God! Just those few words sent me wild. I was feeling so turned on now, I just wanted to see him and f*ck him. It was like a frenzy of lust. My blood was pumping so hard, I was so wet and ready for him, I needed sex and needed it now. 'Can I come over?' I can't believe I have been that forward with him, just inviting myself to his place.

'Maybe…'

'Stop playing games! Seriously. I want to come and sit on your face.'

'Bring all your toys with you and make it within an hour!'

Shit, I need a babysitter. I got on the phone to everyone I knew asking if they could do an hour's sitting for me and I would pay double for the short notice. After securing a babysitter I started to get ready as fast as I could, dancing around my bedroom like a stupid teenager. Double shit, I've had a drink! Can I drive? I'll order a taxi. I can't miss this. I can't *not* see him.

'What are you wearing now?'

'A black slip.'

'Keep it on.'

'But it's cold. I'm going to freeze to death, it's the middle of winter.'

'I don't care.'

'I have left all my heels at work.'

'What do you have?'

'Cowboy boots.' I sat back and waited for him to cancel.

'Put them on!'

The babysitter arrived, so I thanked her and explained that she had nothing to do because both the kids were asleep but to call me if she had any problems. I got in the taxi wearing a big thick winter coat and some brown cowboy boots, no knickers, no bra and my skin was still red from the hot bath. I'd covered myself in perfume and my make-up looked natural; he was getting a real hurried messy version of me tonight.

The taxi pulled up outside his posh house. I looked in the mirror to check that my face looked OK; I was flushed from the bath and the wine and being turned on. I took my coat off and instantly felt freezing cold, but I got out of the taxi and knocked on the door. He opened it and laughed at me. I looked stupid. I laughed with him and we kissed, still laughing. I looked directly into his eyes and told him that I only had an hour and he needed to set his alarm on his phone so that I left in time for my sitter. We set our phones' alarms, put them to one side and headed to the bedroom with my bag of toys.

I emptied them all out onto the bed. He pulled my slip off, revealing my naked body, but left my boots on and pushed me onto the bed. I looked into his eyes and got lost in the moment, time just stopped or I wish it could have. I loved being in these moments with him, we just didn't care about anything – it was so spontaneous and fun.

He wanted to watch me f*ck myself with my vibrator. I'd never done this before, being watched by someone, and this was a massive turn on for him. While I was doing this and watching his reaction he reached for the whip and blindfold. He put the blindfold over my eyes and hit my body with the whip, not being able to see made it more intense. He did this over and over until I made myself cum all over his fancy sheets. He took my hand and guided me to the side of the bed and asked me to kneel down on the floor in front of the mirrors so that we could see each other's naked bodies, He took the blindfold off.

"Now put your vibrator in your pussy and watch yourself."

"Like this?" I sat down on the rabbit and tuned it on.

"Yes, now relax and just go with it."

He then slowly inserted himself into my bottom. I was so shocked and gave out a little yelp, but didn't argue with him. It felt OK, but very full – an unusual sensation. It was quite overwhelming and a bit of a balancing act was needed.

"God I can feel the vibrator vibrating against my cock."

"It feels good?" I asked. Looking into the mirror and seeing him throwing his head back in pure ecstasy, I was taking him to the edge; I loved seeing him fall apart. I screamed out as I was about to come and he pulled me onto the bed and put my mouth to his penis to swallow his cum. To my horror, I was too late and it went up my nose and into my eyes, highly unattractive.

After cleaning up the mess we fell onto the bed laughing and then started to kiss again; we had at least another thirty minutes. I wanted to do it again so I got on top of him and took control. I pinned him to the bed and sat on him. Gyrating slowly, going in and out until I picked up a rhythm and then faster and faster, I f*cked him hard. It's about time Fancy Pants had a taste of his own medicine; I could be controlling in the bedroom too.

After we finished f*cking we went downstairs to the kitchen for a quick drink. I sat on the worktop swinging my legs and grinning at him. He walked over and without warning he was back inside me. It was a funny angle to f*ck but he was doing really well. We kissed hard and then I screamed out, it all happened so fast. It was the most intense orgasm I had ever had, but a gush of water came with it!

"Oh my God!" he shouted. "Mmmmmm, F*CK that feels good!"

"What the f*ck. I'm sorry!" Water was all over him and the floor. I blushed, I didn't know what had just happened; there was so much of it.

"Don't be, you just gushed, squirted, it's an intense orgasm. It's perfectly normal and natural, and very hot!"

"Can you please get me a towel and I'll clean it up."

"Look, don't worry about it, it was very sexy." He looked into my eyes reassuringly and then both our alarms went off at the same time. "Shit, I need to go. You OK cleaning this up yourself?"

"Yes it's fine, get going."

My taxi was waiting outside.

I grabbed my slip and put it on. I gave him a massive hard kiss on the lips and ran toward the door.

"What about all your toys?"

"I'll get them another time, look after them for me." I was out of the door so fast, leaving him standing in the doorway, waving me goodbye. I was already starting to miss him.

I got a text when I got home from him saying 'F*CK ME, that was really good!'

I replied with, 'It will only get better, you sexy f*cker!'

Chapter Eighteen
Relationship Advice

Another week had gone by. I had texted 'Mr Fancy Pants' every day and got nothing back. I was devastated, I really did like him now and there was no denying the fact that I wanted him to be a part of my life.

I bought Christian Carter's book 'Catch Your Man and Keep Him' and signed up to numerous websites to gauge what he might be thinking or feeling or what I had done wrong to make him not want me any more. Texting too much was top of the list; men like to hide in their little man caves when they have been very intimate with a woman and they tend to back off. Apparently, if you smother them, they run for the hills and I had been completely overdoing the texts. I also took advice from my gay friend at work, who in no uncertain terms told me I was wasting my time and that I was being used.

"You need to be assertive and show him that you respect yourself and want someone who's going to be serious!"

"I know, but if I do that he will think I'm up myself won't he?"

"Look, he knows he can get you with a click of his fingers, you will just go running. He has you exactly where he wants you."

"I like him wanting me."

"Yes but you're now just a slag to him, he doesn't respect you."

"How do you know that?"

"Because if he did, you wouldn't be getting treated this way by him."

"How do you know he's just not ready, or he's scared?"

"Because he's a player, I've seen this a million times, come on wake up! Look, watch this." He gave me a video of some relationship advice guru who basically advised people like me that we needed to be strong and confidant and empowered, and, most importantly, be in control.

I finished watching the video and started to text 'Mr User Fancy Pants'. I was cross and angry and confused and wanted to make this text the text from me that he would never forget.

'Dear Mr Twatpants

Ignoring someone is rude and uncalled for.

I have done some thinking, and I am looking for someone who is extraordinary and I deserve to find him. I have a great personality and a loving heart and I will not be treated this way by you or anyone. So unless you man up and ask me out, you can f*ck off. I'm sick of this. It's up to you now!

Love...

Little Miss F*cked Off With Your Behaviour.'

I sent it but as soon as I sent it I felt awful, and mean. I wished I hadn't written it and wanted to retract it, but it was too late. Within minutes of sending the text, I could see it had been read. I waited for his response. The WhatsApp of his picture then disappeared and I couldn't see anything any more. He'd blocked me! Not only had he blocked me on WhatsApp, on Facebook and on

Instagram, everything was gone. In one fell swoop, I was out of his life, deleted.

I told my friend in the office, and he simply said, "I told you so. There is your answer."

F*CK!

Chapter Nineteen
Broke

There are two types of people in this world – Shits and Super-Shits.

Shits are the ones who think that they are doing the right thing and are good people even though they are doing a spectacular job of being selfish and all consuming, but try to look good to others. Super-Shits don't give a f*ck. They do exactly what makes them happy and other people's lives and feelings are never taken into consideration. Everyone is a complete and utter shit of a bastard at some point in their life; doesn't matter if they have religion, education or logic. All human beings mess up.

After my interview I very quickly was re-employed. Having not preformed, needless to say the company was suddenly 'in trouble' and I was made redundant. For years of being nice to this man, there was not even a "Goodbye" or a "Sorry, you won't be able to feed your children this month, I hated his attitude and coldness and lack of self-respect for me, I would never darken his door again.

I was mad, madder than I'd ever been before. In the space of a week, I had been dumped by my f*ck buddy and let go from a job because presumably I wouldn't jump on either of their dicks anytime they click their fingers. To think I cared so much about BOTH of them and wasted SO much time and effort communicating and trying to make them happy.

I dropped the kids off at their dad's house and even though I knew I couldn't afford it I decided to go sit at the end of a bar and get absolutely drunk. It was the only way my head was going to tell me what to do next. I arrived at my best mate's bar, sat down with a massive sigh and felt like I was going to burst into tears.

"Hey, what's up? You look awful."

"Geeeeeemmmm, I've been dumped by Fancy Pants and made redundant for not giving my boss a blow job… I think."

"Oh God. NO… vodka then?"

"Double please!"

"What are you going to do?"

"God knows. I have no savings and bill payments going out next week. I'm literally completely broke."

"Take him to court? Seriously, I've seen the texts from him – you could get him into so much trouble."

"Don't worry; I'm a firm believer in karma."

"Cheers, to vodka!"

"What's happened with Fancy Pants, then? I thought you two were OK, having fun?"

"We were until I took advice from a gay friend and a relationship site video. Now I'm blocked and gone from his life forever. It's just as well; I won't be able to buy naughty underwear, expensive vibrators and hair extensions now."

"Haha. You are unbelievable. I told you to just play it cool with him. Men don't like 'serious'."

"I know, I'm learning fast how small their minds are and how gigantic they think their penises are."

"Just have a break now, no more dating and focus fully on getting a job. Why don't you go part-time and get benefits, have a bit of downtime? You work so hard, have a rest, half of the country are taking the piss working part-time with kids!"

"I might not have a choice, look at my bills, I'm seriously in trouble now. Today I had a call from the Jobcentre about my first appointment. I have to sign on for the first time in my life AND go to a foodbank to feed us." I pulled out all my bills from my bag and showed her how bad things had become. I was planning to pay things off at the end of the month but I was only on a week's notice, so I couldn't afford, literally, to even wipe my ass.

"What's this letter for? Jesus! They are going to start taking things from your house?"

"Yep, next week the bailiffs are going to enter my house and take out whatever they see fit, to pay off some bills. I'll tell them to take the sofa. It's been pissed on by the dog this week anyway and it will save me calling the council, they can take it with pleasure. They can have the f*cking dog too!"

Gem laughed and poured me another vodka. "Here, this is on me, cheers." I downed it in one.

"I will be OK, I always am. This is a life lesson about men who think their knobs rule the world. Just wait until I get back up and f*ck them right up the ass!"

"That's the spirit, lady. So, what progress have you had so far job hunting, have you found anything yet?"

"Don't laugh OK, but I think I'm in with a chance doing telesales. The company is just around the corner from my house and the job's part-time. It would be a stop-gap until I get back into management."

"What's it selling?"

"I can't tell you, I'm embarrassed."

"Come on, I'm your best mate, I won't judge you."

"You laugh and I will kill you."

"Go on, tell me."

"Minibuses!" We looked at each other and burst out laughing. I couldn't for a second imagine the change from working for a global corporation in a management role, to phoning people, asking if they wanted to buy a minibus. This was my worst nightmare, but it would put food on the table for me and my kids, warmth and the occasional large glass of wine to cope with my shit existence of a life.

I turned to Gem and did a pretend phone call, and she role played back.

"Hello, this is Miss Fancy Pants. We have a range of spectacular minibuses in all colours, shapes and sizes, super shiny and able to fit at least twelve screaming brats in, just what every person ever dreamed of. So, do we have a deal? If you don't buy one from me, I will hunt you down and run you over!"

"I will take five."

Pissed out of my face after five double vodka and cokes, I'm feeling in a lighter mood and determined to take over the world. Tomorrow I WLL have a new job and everything will be OK – I am invincible! And I don't need a MAN! In fact, I'm starting to hate them and hope that evolution will wipe them all out and replace them with a new species that doesn't think there's a connection between dick and brain.

Chapter Twenty
The Drunken Date with the Dog!

Stood up! Not even a phone call. I looked like such an idiot in the restaurant and couldn't afford more than a glass of wine; this was supposed to be his treat. I am so drunk right now after buying a cheap bottle of red on the way home and I deserve to be.

It's come to this, alone and drunk with my dog as the only living thing I can get a date with that actually remotely likes me!

I haven't had sex in ages. Why can't I think of something else instead of penis anyway? What's the fascination with it? They are ugly and smell, they make an awful mess sometimes, they can really hurt you too (if you're not careful). They should come with a warning 'don't go near, they only want to squirt you in the eye or up your nose'. I've had a black eye from one before, they are dangerous. God, I should write a book – Fifty Shades of Penis by Mrs Wish She Could Be Fancy Pants. Oh, here we go again, I'm still thinking about him. STOPPPP IT! You know, whenever I start talking to a man, you can tell that the lights are on but only the penis is listening. I don't know why I bother trying to get a boyfriend; they all just want a shag.

The information about dating is overwhelming. Hook-ups just for sex, Swingers' websites for threesomes,

Match, POF, Tinder – it's all horseshit! None of it works, well not for me anyway. Maybe I'm just not ready? Why am I so confused? If anyone actually does like me and shows commitment, I get freaked out, is this because I like 'Mr Fancy Pants', or that the thought of spending my Sunday mornings in B&Q looking at decorating patterns scares the life out of me?

Seriously, most people I know who are in a relationship are bored shitless, they stay for kids and money but are not true to themselves. I should know, half of them have tried to shag me. Sex is only good when you have a connection with one person that you can trust, then you can do all this crazy stuff with them to spice it up if that's what turns you both on. You shouldn't have to hide and cheat and lie, just find a sexually compatible partner and go for it. F*ck like crazy, do it everywhere, in every way.

Be an animal, goddam it. It's OK for you, my knicker chewing dog, you smelly thing, go get a shower. I love you, but you stink and I'm sick of you shitting all over my house. What would you do if I had a shit in front of you? It's not nice, STOP IT! I can't afford to keep getting carpets cleaned all the time; I'm a poor single mum. Gemma is right; you DO look like one of my ex boyfriends, oh my word, I went out with someone who looked like my dog too, this gets worse.

I'm SO depressed! Dog look-a-like dater, with no money, no job, broken down car and you've destroyed my best pair of French knickers. How are you not dead? I want you to die right now. No, I don't, YES I do. Stop chewing my knickers, weirdo dog.

And what's with sniffing other dogs' bottoms anyway? It's disgusting, and the humping? I'm a bit jealous if I'm honest; wish it was that easy for me to get a shag from a man. Jump on and f*ck off, no talking – perfect. Most people, if they are honest, just want a good seeing to and no conversation afterwards, no complications. I'm coming back as a dog in my next life!

Screw men anyway, I don't need one, I can go solo. God gave us fingers for a reason and made a man to invent batteries.

Helicopter head. RIGHT-SLEEP! Goodnight diary, good night dog. F*ck off world, you total bitch!... I'm so sad and so lost.

Chapter Twenty-one
You Light Me Up!

Month had gone by and I was sitting at my desk doing my pointless job. I had almost finished for the day when my phone pinged loudly, startling me. I quickly finished what I was doing and packed up. I decided to leave opening my message until I was on my way out of the office.

My body froze and I stopped in my tracks; a picture of 'Mr Fancy Pants' was on my WhatsApp, smiling at me, laying down on his sofa at home. He looked washed out but sexy as hell. His hair had been cut and he was wearing a casual jumper. I'd not seen him in a jumper before, but more importantly, I'd not seen him in ages. It had been over two months since I'd had a message or a call; I thought I was never going to hear from him again. He obviously could see that I had opened the message and not replied so he sent another text. 'How are you?'

'Fantastic, thank you." All lies. I have a shit job, no money, have not had hair extensions or tans in months so as to look amazing for him IF he contacted me. All my best underwear had been chewed by the dog and I still think about you every day and I have been completely miserable without you.

'I haven't heard from you for over two months, why are you texting me?'

'Have you met anyone?'

'Have you?' I wasn't going to answer him, why should I play this game?

'I want to see you again, can you come over?'

'Why? What? Now?'

'Yes, later today.'

'So you have basically called me because you want to have sex and you've run out of people to contact or you've f*cked everyone off? I'm a last resort?'

'No, I do really like you.'

This was the first time he had said that to me and because it was, it felt like he might be telling the truth. It made me feel like I was right back where we had left off but I was still really mad at him for deleting me out of his life with no explanation, it was just brutal.

I decided to call him; I would be able to tell if he was telling the truth by the sound of his voice. "Fancy pants, seriously, do you think I am little miss dial a f*ck? You finished with me over two months ago, so what the f*ck are you doing? Have you run out of options in your little black book, no one else wants to f*ck you? Is that it?"

"Don't shout…my head hurts, I was out last night!"

"Ah ha, you're on a downer after a drinking session and need a pick me up, cheers! I think you could quite easily learn how to go f*ck yourself, you total knobhead!"

"It's not like that. Look, you just scared me. We have so much fun, come over, I do really want to see you."

"No, I have plans with Gem, we are out later, seeing the new Fifty Shades movie."

"I've been told it's tame, come over here and I will show you fifty shades of f*cking better!"

"I can't let my friend down, sorry."

I immediately wanted to cancel and re-arrange just so I could run into his arms, stupid stupid girl. God I'd missed him so much and his fancy massive dick, even if right now it was attached to his head.

"What time does the movie finish? Maybe after?"

God, he really does want to see me, perhaps I should let down my guard and go. I'm only being stubborn to make him know he's been a shit to me, and that he can't just pick back up anytime he wants me.

"You still have all my toys at your house or have you thrown them away?"

"Yeah, I've still got them. What have you been using instead, a rolling pin?"

"Who the hell do you think I am? F*cking Mary Berry? I hope you haven't been using them with other women." He ignored my comment completely.

"Another reason for you to come over, come on, I want you. Your toys are expensive and you must want them back."

After a long pause I just gave in, I couldn't help myself. "Look, I will try but it won't be until late, can I text you later?"

He said OK, and that he was looking forward to seeing me again. I didn't know what had just happened but I found myself singing at the top of my voice in my car, feeling like I was flying. We had had no contact in over two months and instantly I was alive again. It was like I'd been dead and someone had just given me a massive dose of adrenaline.

I got home, got the kids ready to go to their dad's house and danced around the house, making them laugh. I ran round after them, tickling them and blowing raspberries on their tummies. I was always so happy when he was in my life, it affected everything; I had been lost without him.

"What's happened, Mummy, why are you so happy?"

"Someone I like likes me back!"

"Mummy, you're so silly!" I gave my boy the biggest kiss and cuddle and spun him around in the air.

"Yes, I am, darling, but I'm the best mummy in the world, right?"

"You're just too silly, Mummy."

I got ready to go out with Gem, and wouldn't shut up about it all the time we were drinking and getting ready. She couldn't believe he'd come back to me, we both thought I'd well and truly messed it up.

"After the movie, just go to him; look how happy you are, just take the risk, and take the chance and go. What do you have to lose?"

"I love him, don't I? I can't get away from it."

"Yeah, you are 100% CRAZY in love, I've never seen you like this before, you are so happy that he's back. Just be careful, OK? I'm still not sure if he's using you."

We arrived at the pictures and had a few drinks before we went in and I was having fun, but all I could think about was what comes after the movie? I hoped that time would pass quickly so I could be with him again. We came out of the pictures after watching semi hot sex scenes that I could write better. It had been a bit of a disappointment like he said it would be. I turned my phone on and I had a message from him. Delighted, I opened the message, my heart pounding. Perhaps he would be asking me when I was setting off.

'I can't do tonight now.'

I showed Gem the text; she shook her head, put her arm around me and we headed to the pub to get horribly, horribly drunk.

Chapter Twenty-two
Poker Nights and Lesbians

I phoned in sick today. I had had the weekend off but I couldn't get out of bed because I was so depressed. I needed to make things happen, make my life better than it was now. I was not this person, I hated going into work. I hated that I had less hair than my grandma and I needed to break this cycle of dating and sleeping with people that didn't really want me.

I had to put an action plan together. I always made things happen.

1. Update CV and send it everywhere and find a well-paid full time job that I knew I would love.
2. Get a spray tan, I'll feel better.
3. Book an appointment to get my hair extensions put back in.
4. Get out of bed and eat something before I die.
5. NEVER sleep with 'Mr Fancy Pants' again, and ask him for my toys back.

I texted him before doing anything else and I asked him for my things back. I was quite blunt; I didn't want to get into a conversation with him. We arranged a meeting in a week's time as he was going away with work.

'What are you doing today?'

'Day off, then busy all day, so I can't really talk.' I had been sitting in the bath for an hour doing absolutely nothing but feeling sorry for myself, just wanting him to leave me alone, so I could get on with being miserable.

'When are you getting a lesbian for the threesome we were talking about?'

'I told you. I logged on to POF and pretended to be gay for you for a week. I talked to lesbians day in day out and none of them wanted me. I have a hard time pulling men let alone a woman! They could tell I was not gay, it's too difficult, plus it didn't turn me on like I thought it might.'

'I don't care about any of that, just find someone if you want to see me again. I want to watch you being f*cked by a woman.'

'Look, I know you should try everything once, but I don't think it's going to work for me, sorry. I'm sure you can find someone else who will do it, if you haven't already.'

'I want to watch you being licked by a woman and me f*cking you at the same time.' I paused and didn't text for ten minutes. I didn't know what to say.

'Would you f*ck her too?'

'No, both of us would be doing it to you.'

'Why are you being so pushy? I mean, I know you're confident and direct with me but you're being a bit mean, what's wrong?' He avoided the question.

'I'm having a poker night in a few weeks and I thought you might want to come, dress up in an outfit and serve chips. I want you to do this with a lesbian so find someone before then. I will pay for the outfits.'

'What kind of outfit?' He sent me a picture of a woman in a black and white 'bunny girl' outfit, very revealing and low cut, with fishnet tights. It was sexy, not much to it.

I thought to myself, does this mean he wants me to meet his friends, and is this a step forward if he wants me to do that? I told him it was an exciting idea but I would have to think about it and get back to him.

I called 'Mr Under The Table' to ask for advice on what to do. I told him all about the text. "So what do you think?"

"If you go to that party, you will get raped!"

"I'm sorry – what?"

"Dressing up as a bunny girl to serve chips and for him to let his friends f*ck you one by one, or together, is what I imagine will happen."

"He is not like that, he wouldn't let anything bad happen to me."

"All he's ever done are nasty things to you. I hate this man, tell me where he lives please. I want to go smash his face in."

"No, calm down, honestly I think he just wants a bit of fun. I'd just be helping out at the party. Really he is a nice man deep down, I've seen it."

"Why do you always have his back, always stand up for him? If a man asks you to do something like this, he has no respect for you at all."

"Really?"

"Yes really, and if you go, you could end up raped or dead! Promise me you won't go. Please stay away from him, he's bad news and this is the worst thing you have told me about him. The lesbian thing is HOT. I'd love to do that with a woman too, it's quite normal. You should try it but not with him. Please take these stupid rose-tinted glasses off, he doesn't love you and never has, you are his prostitute and it's destroying you, you are worth more!"

We talked about it for hours and I shed some tears. He made me laugh and told me to get up and sort myself out, that I was better than this and I'd just lost my confidence, allowing myself to be controlled by the world's largest walking penis.

I told Gem and she set off in her car to go punch him in the face so I had to get in my car and go and stop her. Today I realised that I have good friends and I should really start to listen to them, but I knew I wouldn't.

Chapter Twenty-three
The Brother and the Baby Sitter's Father

Valentine's Day has been as bad as every other one for the last six years of my life, no flowers, no chocolates, no romantic meals and no shag. The only thing going near my vagina today was a metal penis whilst I was having a smear test at the clinic. I'm all for kinky but metal inside me, widening my cervix open was not my thing. I was clear for STDs and having my repeat bloods done today.

Laying on my back with my legs wide open, my thoughts drifted to dickhead of the year 'Mr Fancy Pants'. Gosh, how long has it been since I had been exposed like this? If he were here now he probably would have me and the nurse making out and him taking us both with his wicked voodoo magic charm.

I wonder who has the pleasure of his penis tonight. I suddenly felt sick at the thought of him being with another woman, and tried to shake him out of my head. The only way I could comfort my thoughts was to imagine him with a really overweight, spotty, smelly, sweaty, stupid person – who sounded like Peter Kay.

I'd only been out of work a short time before securing that dreadful job working in telesales selling minibuses, and that included wearing a uniform! I'd never felt so unbelievably stupid in my life, apart from the time when I realised I'd married an idiot. I'd started to receive tax credits and housing benefit and we were able to eat better again. I did a massive food shop and filled the cupboards and I was no longer being reminded that 'Daddy is doing better'. The sofa and TV had been taken by bailiffs, so I had nothing to sit on or to watch but I was being positive, things would get better. I have my iPhone and YouTube; who watches TV anyway?

The kids were going to their dad's house tonight for the weekend and I was going to have the first drink in well over a week. Since it was Valentine's Day I treated myself to a selection of drinks to make cocktails with, and fully intending to stuff my face with tiramisu. I'd had lots of messages from friends and a sweet message from my dad telling me they loved me and to keep my chin up, and that I wouldn't be single for ever; there is a pot for every lid!

I got home, had a bubble bath and glass of wine and listened to the 'Top 40 Love Songs of All Time' CD. Coming downstairs to my empty house, I turned the volume up, dropped my towel and danced around the kitchen naked, making cocktails and singing into a rolling-pin 'microphone', singing the lyrics to "What's that coming over the hill, is it a monster? No, is it a minibus?"

Pissed and lonely, making cocktails for one on Valentine's Day, proud owner of nothing but shit loads of debt and a rusty old car. My ex-husband was so tight that the day I left him he took my wedding rings off me, and I'd bought the bloody things! I could have sold them to eat this month. Was it not enough that he got the house? I hope wherever the rings are, they accidentally gets stuck right up his asshole and Golam finds them in the night and pulls them out.

A message came through on my phone; it was a waving emoji from a random. Oh here we go, who's stalking me now? Some sado on Valentine's Day. I'd had a few to drink but had to look twice because it appeared to be a relative of 'Mr Fancy Pants'. I texted 'Hello, do I know you?'

'You messaged me a few weeks ago.'

'I did?' I looked at his picture; he was fat and ugly but had the same eyes as 'Mr Fancy Pants'. Jesus – was this his brother?

'What did the message say?'

'Call me!'

'Errmmm, oh, sorry, there has been some mistake, sorry.' I had messaged the wrong person.

'Ah. No worries, I thought I was in luck for a minute.'

I didn't reply for a good thirty minutes, but instead of leaving it at that (which I should have done), the alcohol and curiosity took over. 'Are you 'Mr Fancy Pants's brother?'

'Yeah I am. How do you know him?'

'We kind of dated for a while but it's all over now, he dumped me.'

'Really? He's never mentioned you. When did you see him?'

'I'd been seeing him for over six months, off and on, more off than on. All we seemed to do was fall out.'

'What days did you see him?'

I thought it was a bit of an odd question, but answered it anyway. 'Usually a Friday or a Sunday night, a few times a month, sometimes not even that.'

He put a lot of laughing face emojies on the next message.

'What's so funny?'

'Nothing, you need to get over him and move on.'

'He's given me no choice, I appear to be blocked from everything. I'm pretty sure he thinks I'm a psycho bitch.'

'My brother is a very private man, and basically I can't tell you anything about him because to be honest he doesn't tell me much nowadays. Hey, come on a date with me, you're stunning, he must be mad!'

'Ha. I don't think so, not the thing to do at all but thank you for the offer. I'd feel terrible if he even knew we were texting, please don't tell him, OK?'

'So, did you two have good sex? I taught him everything he knows.''

'What? You two had sex together? Haha.'

'lol.'

(I'm pretty sure that's not an appropriate thing to be discussing with you, 'Mr Ugly F*cker'.)

'Come on, what did he do that was so good?'

'We had a few passionate moments on his kitchen table and I think that's taking it way too far now. I've had quite a lot to drink.'

'Yeah, I've had a few women on that table.'

'What do you mean? Did you used to own the table before him?' There was no answer to this. All sorts went through my head. Is there some sick twisted f*cked up shit going on, or has he used his brother's fancy house a few times to pull women?

It was like talking to 'Mr Fancy Pants'; he was soft and gentle at first then full on filth and pushiness. I was starting to see a pattern, a worrying explanation for his behaviour. If he'd had this monkey as any kind of role model growing up, then no wonder he was the way he was.

'Make my day, and show me your pussy.'

'What! F*ck off! Are you for real?'

'Come on, what better offer are you going to get on Valentine's Day? Can you video chat? I want to see you.' I thought to myself, at what point in these texts did I give the impression I was interested in him or that I was desperate?

'What sort of things do you like men doing to you? Do you squirt? I think the wetter the better.'

I didn't answer but thought I'd be smart and try to get some information out of this idiot before I blocked him or reported him to the police. 'So how is your brother? I haven't seen him in months.' My heart was pounding, please don't tell me he's got a girlfriend and is blissfully happy.

'I don't know, I've not spoken to him for a while. I hardly ever see him. Do you use toys?'

'Why don't you see him, are you not close or both just busy?' I knocked a cocktail down my neck in the time it took him to work out the answer.

'I stay with him sometimes, I work away a lot. Come on, video chat with me.'

'No, I'm not video chatting with you – look I really like your brother, OK?' I thought that would be the end to the texts but he was not giving up.

'Well he's not interested in you, is he, or you wouldn't be blocked. Honestly, get over him, go out there and have some fun.'

'Come on, send me a naked picture.'

'Ha. I will send you a naked picture if you send me one'. That should do it, he will shit himself and f*ck off!

I put my phone down, turned my music up and danced around my house again, naked. My head was spinning after drinking three quarters of every bottle of spirits I had been mixing; I was feeling rather drunk.

I made one more drink, and with tiramisu and my laptop, went upstairs to my bed to watch a movie before I fell asleep. My phone beeped with a message on WhatsApp. It was him again. For f*ck's sake will you not just f*ck off now? It was a video recording, (he'd decided to send this rather than send me a pic). I could see the image of a half-naked man sitting on the side of a bath and my body froze. Do I delete it or watch it? I can't believe this is happening to me, even 'Mr Fancy Pants' wouldn't do anything like this.

I got my spoon and started eating my tiramisu and pressed 'play'. After watching him wank off and crying out my name and cum going all over the place, I realised I had just reached a new level of f*cked up.

'Now, your turn, you said you would and you should always keep your word.'

That's what 'Mr Fancy Pants' always said too. Without any thought process, I did what I was told.

I ran to the toilet and threw up. My days of tiramisu were over. I would never be able to face either the dessert or 'Mr Fancy Pants' ever again. It's a good job he'd dumped me, I'm an awful human being, and really messed up over him.

Unfortunately, the photo did not just go to 'Mr Ugly F*cker', it went to a few people, one being my babysitter's dad. How I did this was completely beyond me. I had a very angry voicemail waiting for me when I returned to bed, and I wanted to die.

I'm going to end up on Crime Watch as the local flasher!

Happy Valentine's day to me!

Chapter Twenty-four
The Last Time

I was walking the dog with the kids when my phone beeped. I let the dog off the lead and the kids went to play in the park. I ignored my phone for at least half an hour. A really attractive man in the park walking his dog kept looking over at me and made me blush. My dog was playing with his dog, so I walked over and we began chatting. To our horror , my dog jumped on the back of his dog and started ruthlessly humping. Our desperate attempts to free his dog got worse as they kept running off so they could shag somewhere else and not be stopped.

"At least someone is having a good time, right?" I blurted out, laughing.

He did not look amused. "She's not been done yet!"

"Oh my God, I'm so sorry." I ran over to my dog and pulled him off his dog and picked him up, walking away from the man in complete embarrassment, carrying a panting horny little dog with his willy sticking out! The man and his dog quickly disappeared.

I opened my bag, got my phone out and looked at the WhatsApp that had beeped before my sex mad dog was unleashed. 'How's Little Miss Cheeky? Still coming to get your toys?'

I replied with, 'Just throw them in the bin.'

'Don't be silly, they are expensive toys. They're here for you to collect, do you want to pick them up tonight? I will be in at seven p.m.'

'If I come round, we will end up f*cking.'

'And the problem with that is?'

'I don't have a lesbian to bring as requested, and I've been ignored again.'

'You come out with complete shit, that's why, and I've been busy, I told you. I want you to wear a miniskirt, will you do that?'

'I don't think so, all my miniskirts are work clothes, how about a short black dress?'

'Wear that then with no knickers. I will get the wine!' Bloody hell, that's a first, 'Mr Fancy Tight As F*ck Never Taken Me Out Or Bought Anything For Me Pants' is actually buying me some wine!

It was very strange going back to see him again. I felt rather nervous and extremely guilty after all the issues I had had with his brother. Getting ready was not as exciting as it used to be and my feelings for him were not as intense any more. I suppose I'd started to get over him.

My car was in the garage so I got a lift from a friend who didn't want to kill him. She pulled up outside his house and he came to answer the door, and gave us both a big smile. I kissed her goodbye, said, "Wish me luck," and she was gone.

He was wearing a smart dark blue shirt – he looked so amazing. His dress sense tonight was good and the smell of him made it hard for me to control myself. All the feelings that I thought had drifted away came back and I was right back to where I'd left off – I still loved him. I was a little bit drunk as I'd had half a bottle of wine (Dutch courage) to go and see him. I looked OK in my dress but didn't feel sexy like I used to, and the energy around us didn't make me feel special; it was guilt.

We looked into each other's eyes, and I found myself leaning in to him to kiss him. It wasn't passionate like it used to be and he pulled away from me. I felt the old familiar lurch in my stomach – he was talking control. I slipped my dress down off my shoulders so he could see my breasts, and he started to suck them hard. I let my dress fall to the floor. Still standing against the counter he began to play with me. Pushing me off him and leading me to the table he pushed me down on my back, pulled up a chair and went down on me, but not looking at me all the time like he used to, and being quite rough. Christ, I could feel my body shaking, I never wanted it to stop. Pulling me back up I banged my head on his kitchen lamp, we laughed and then he pushed me to my knees. I did as I was told.

"Suck my cock." I put his penis in my mouth and looked at him, making sounds as if I loved it and hoping for the best. I looked at him with his penis in my mouth and started to laugh. I can't believe I have got the giggles right now.

"Shut the f*ck up and suck."

"I can't stop laughing. I'm sorry, I will try again. Hahahaha. I'm sorry, I think we need to give it up as a bad idea, I can't do it!"

He had a poker face tonight, I couldn't read him at all. He picked me up and I was back on the table facing him. He thrust himself inside me; my body was like a wave on the kitchen table, moaning and twisting to his every command. He stopped and pulled me to the edge of the table, now putting at least three fingers inside and working his magic. I screamed out and then his kitchen table was soaking wet. I covered my face with my hands - he's going to have to buy a new kitchen table! Smirking and quickly cleaning up the wetness, he then flipped me over so my bottom was facing him and he thrust inside me again. I told him to film it, "I want to watch this back when we are done", I said. I could hear him reaching for his phone and the record button being pressed. Sweet Lord, the sex was unreal. He was f*cking me the hardest he'd ever done, with no mercy and didn't stop when I couldn't take any more. We both came but this time he came inside me, something he'd never done before, and somewhere he'd never cum before. I heard him gasp in surprise that he'd cum so hard. It was all over very quickly; just like my dog in the park today. It was definitely just a quick f*ck, the 'connection' had gone.

He offered me a glass of wine and I got dressed and sat down at the now clean and dry kitchen table and smiled at him. He got dressed and stood across the room from me and I could tell he wanted to talk about something. To my amazement, he started to talk about his brother and that he was supposed to have come to fix something in his house but never turned up. I instantly felt sick – how the f*ck am I going to handle this? He never talks to me about his family or friends or anything at all really, what's going on? Does he know?

He talked about sharing women, in the context that it's OK to do so and perfectly normal. I asked how that was normal exactly so he spoke about orgies and best mates sharing women; is this what he had in mind for me next? Had 'Mr Under The Table' been right after all?

I looked all around the room, anywhere except his face. He could see I was clearly uncomfortable with the way the conversation was going. The guilt was too much for me to cope with. I couldn't lie to someone I cared about, even if it meant losing him for ever.

"Look, I have something to tell you. I messaged your brother on Facebook by mistake one night when I was really drunk whilst trying to find you." He messaged me back and flirted with me and I told him I had been seeing you and that I'd messaged him by mistake. He sent me a video of himself wanking and I sent a photo back to him of me naked."

I just blurted it out without thinking about my words; I'd been desperate to tell him for so long. I'd written letters but never posted them and typed a million texts and deleted them, not that he'd get them because I was blocked anyway. I explained that I'd never met his brother and that I'd ended the communication very quickly, telling him how much I cared about you. I explained that I told him never to contact me again.

To my surprise, he laughed. "Next time I see him, I will take the piss out of him," he said. Was this his defence or did he genuinely not give a shit?

I got off my chair to move to him and hold him and tell him how much I cared about him and that I was sorry, but he pushed me away. "Look we have had fun, but we probably won't ever sleep together again." He reached into his pocket and pulled out his phone and began to call a taxi.

Nothing else was said between us. I gathered my things; I didn't look at him again but walked away and out of the door before I burst into tears. I cried in the taxi all the way home and all night, with no sleep.

I must have texted him a million times saying sorry and that I loved him. His reply was that I had nothing to apologise for, that it was his fault for being a dickhead too. The pain was unbearable.

Tonight had been a revenge f*ck! No wonder his behaviour of late had been so disrespectful.

Goodbye 'Mr Fancy Pants'. I'm so sorry. I know that you already knew.

Chapter Twenty-five
Broken – Part one

I could see flash lights in the distance getting closer and closer and knew this time I was in serious trouble.

Naked, tied to a low tree branch with my hands above my head, freezing cold and stinking of alcohol, I was not the perfection of beauty; I was a mess. The flash lights were shining in my eyes now, so I had to look away and I could clearly hear a voice in the distance.

"I'm OK," I shouted, hardly able to find my voice. Two police officers flashed their lights towards me, thereby showing my naked body hanging from the tree, and they gasped in shock.

"It's not what it looks like."

"What's your name, love? We are going to get you down."

I told them my name, and one of the officers spoke on his radio to inform the police station that they had arrived at the crime scene. I was helped down and was given a blanket and my clothes, then escorted down the hill to the police car, in silence. I was shaking so much, I found it hard to keep my balance. I sat in the back of the police car and one officer prepared to take a statement. How the heck was I going to get out of this one, and had they seen 'Mr Pissed Out Of His Face' who'd fallen asleep on the park bench?

When the light was turned on in the car, and the police officer turned around to me to take the statement, my jaw nearly fell on the floor, it was the same officer who had rescued me from 'Mr Strawberry Psycho' several months earlier. "I see you naked more than I see my own wife, young lady! Hello again."

"Hello, officer," I blushed scarlet. "I did listen to your advice, this is nothing like last time, and I'm not a flasher. We were being 'creative'. He's on a park bench passed out up there somewhere, will one of you go check that he's OK?"

"So, what happened this time?"

"I was getting him to act out one of my fantasies and halfway through, he went for a wee and fell asleep on a park bench nearby. I'm afraid we'd had quite a bit to drink."

"So, your fantasy was to be tied to a tree, naked?"

"Well, yes, it's one of them." I blushed again. "But no one was around or could see what we were doing!"

"Miss, it's illegal to have sex in a public place, any time of the day, anywhere in the world."

"I know but at one a.m. in the morning, we didn't think it would be so public. I mean, come on, who walks their dog at that time?"

"The person who called this in does apparently." I looked at him as if to say 'come on, give me a break'.

"It was just a bit of fun, I'm so sorry, it won't happen again."

"This is your last warning. If I have to come out to you again and you're naked or you've put yourself in a dangerous position, I will arrest you! Now I'm taking you home and I don't want to see you again."

He got on the radio and told them it was just kids and they had run off, left the other officer to deal with my drunken date and took me home. He looked at me through the mirror and gave me that same look my parents give me when they are disappointed with me, which is always ten times worse than words. I got out of the car, let myself into the house and looked in the mirror. I was a mess, a disgrace lost and broken hearted.

It had been months since the last time I had seen 'Mr Fancy Pants' and all I had done was drink and smoke and not eat. At every opportunity I was out, anything to avoid the pain in my head from the heartbreak. I was punishing myself for what I had done and tonight had been a wild attempt at having sex to get over him, but it had gone horribly wrong.

I had a shower, got into bed and began to text the only person who would talk some sense into me. If she knew what I was up to, she would forgive me but talk to me in such a way that I never would forget that I had to sort myself out.

'Hey, I know it's really late, but I'm in trouble. I'm in the worst mess I've ever been in and I need you, can I come and visit? Tomorrow?'

A good hour passed until I got a message from her. 'I was expecting this, I'll make the spare room bed up.'

'Thank you, love you.'

'I love you too, but let me sleep and f*ck off.'

The journey was going to take at least nine hours in the car. I was taking the dog for company and had arranged to have regular breaks and chats with friends to keep me going until I arrived at my destination. This was my first ever road trip after passing my driving test, and

I knew it was just what I needed to clear my head and to think about my life, try to gain perspective.

My brother took the piss out of my Facebook post saying I'd never make it. 'Mr Star Wars' wished me luck and went through my checklist to make sure I had done everything needed before setting off.

"Let's do things in your order of priority, cigarettes?"

"Check!"

"Vibrator?"

"Hell yes!"

"Give me the iPhone app to help you out with that."

"Sending it now."

"Petrol, air in your tyres, oil and water checked?"

"Shit, no. On it!"

"Your brother is right; you're never going to make it."

I programmed the satnav in my car, went to my local garage and they did everything for me. I didn't even know how to pop the bonnet when I first got my car; admittedly, I was a bit useless sometimes when it came to practical things. All set, I began my journey and felt positive that at the end of this road trip, I would come back home and be magically fixed and 'me' again.

An hour into the journey, I was bored and so I stopped at the services for a coffee and texted 'Mr Star Wars' to let him know I was ready to try out the lush while I had a bit of time in the car. It can't be that powerful, it's a tiny little thing that you insert inside you, what's the worst that could happen?

Just before setting back off on my journey I texted to tell him to set it off and unleash the madness!

'Are you sure this is safe, you'll be driving.'

'Yeah, come on, it'll be fun, go for it.'

'OK, ready, steady – GO!'

I waited a while and then looked between my legs – nothing was happening. Was it broken? Just my luck, I bet 'Mr Fancy Pants' had been experimenting with it and f*cked it up for me.

'Nothing's happening.'

'Well I'm following the instructions, it should be working.'

'Hang on a minute, I've got a call, can I put you on hold for a second?'

'Sure, I'll wait.'

My mum was calling me; she had the kids so I thought it better not to ignore her. She certainly picks her timing.

"Hello, Mum, everything OK? Kids OK?"

"Yes, everything's fine darling, it's just, I've been sitting doing the ironing in the kitchen, and the washing machine keeps going on and off every few minutes, is it faulty?"

I paused for a few minutes, and then realised that I had given 'Mr Star Wars' the app for the washing machine and not the vibrator.

Chapter Twenty-six
Broken – Part two

I had been driving for three hours and arrived at Gretna Green services, watching all these silly people who flock here to get married. I had become so negative about love. I pulled in and grabbed some dinner and a strong coffee. I was feeling so tired already and still had a three hour drive ahead of me. Turning my phone on, I checked my emails and messages. I had a notification from the NHS to say that all my test results were back and were OK. This was great news. 'Mr Fancy Pants' hadn't given me a life-threatening disease.

I had two emails about interviews for amazing jobs with great prospects and a message from my good friend, responding to my urgent call when I'd had my encounter with the police. He would make Freud look stupid; he just seems to understand most things about human emotions. I had messaged him about my issues, and he had said I had to call him urgently to discuss things. I got back in my car and made the call to 'Mr Philosopher' – always full of answers, and most of the time, completely right.

"Hey, you, you told me to call. Is now a good time? I'm travelling up to Scotland, you're on speaker in the car."

"Yeah, I can talk. To be honest, I'm relieved that you have called, I'm very worried."

"Because of this guy I have been seeing?"

"That and your behaviour. You're completely out of control."

"My heart's broken. It's broken and I can't fix it."

"The only way to get over a broken heart is by giving yourself time, time to have space and reflect on what's just happened. Carrying on dating and looking to fill that space will only make things worse, and you will feel empty. Believe me, I have been there."

"Wait a minute, guys feel like this too? I just thought they got on with it and moved on or went out and shagged loads of women."

"Yeah, some go out shagging and never attaching again, never letting anyone in. Others feel the pain immensely. I had to put a pound in a jar every time I mentioned her name, I was broke! My mates made me do it. You should do it. I'm sick of hearing this f*cking man's name!"

"Mr Fancy Pants is the love of my life. I'm never going to meet anyone I connect with or love as much, in my lifetime. He's the first person I have truly fallen for and could actually say, without even having to think, that I'd do anything to make sure he was safe and happy. For the first time in my life, apart from my children, he comes before me."

"OK, I'm going to do something for you today, and you need to let me know that you are strong enough to deal with this and you have time to listen, because this has to stop and it has to stop now."

"What do you mean?" I was concerned about how his tone had changed and how serious he had become.

"I'm going to get you to see the real situation of what's going on. I'm going to help you to take the rose tinted glasses off and be logical, but you need to really listen to me and take this on board."

"OK, I can try." I lit a cigarette and opened a can of Iron Brew, and sat back. Thankfully the traffic was heavy so we weren't moving fast.

"Love comes in many forms; it's unpredictable, it's crazy and it can make you feel like you are the only two people alive. It can get you so high that you feel like it's a drug to you, but equally it can crush you so hard you believe that you won't ever get back up. You are at the end of love's cycle, you are broken and about to be crushed."

"I'm trying to stay positive, really I am. I'm putting plans in place to make my life better."

"Do you want my advice?"

"Yes."

"Then please listen." (His tone was now very soft and gentle.)

"I have known you a long time. I have seen you get married, watched you bring your children up and looked after your husband when he needed you the most. You're a good woman, with a massive heart, and that's your problem. You care too much for other people, and you love too hard. You're bat shit crazy sometimes, but only people who really know you see that that's OK. This man who you've been seeing has been so out of character for you. How the hell you have not seen him for what he is is beyond me, but, my darling, I'm so sorry to have to tell you this, this is going to be so hard but he doesn't love you and he has never loved you. It hasn't even crossed his mind. You have been used as his prostitute (for free, might I add) for a year."

"How do you know he's never felt anything? You don't know him. I have seen the way he looks at me and the way we are together. He's shown some interested in my life, granted it's not been much but we don't see each other very often."

"OK, so he's never taken you out on a date? You have been sleeping with each other for twelve months, right?" I went silent and didn't respond.

"Has he ever asked you about your children, your job, your family or your friends?" I stayed silent.

"How many times has he made you cry? More times than he's made you happy? Has he ever supported you emotionally?"

"Yes actually, twice, once when told him I was sick, and my first Christmas without the kids he was there for me because he knew I was lonely; he has a heart! I have seen kindness in him, really I have."

"Why are you sticking up for someone who won't even return your calls or messages? Does someone who loves you say to you, "Get round to mine in ten minutes if you want a shag," or "I want you to f*ck another man and film it and send it to me," or "Host a poker night for me and serve chips," or "Get a lesbian to have a threesome or I won't sleep with you again," or "Stick a rolling pin up your f*cking fanny, stick anything up it and send me a pic, I won't show any of my mates, I promise. Oh and, I think it's funny that you will do anything I tell you to do." WTF! COME ON, WAKE UP! I remember everything you tell me. he's a sociopath; he controls you and has no empathy. He doesn't think he's doing anything wrong and so you feel you are the one who's screwing it all up."

"Right, OK, I see where you're coming from, but look at the flip side; what about me and the way I behave around him? I slept with him on the first date, I continued to sleep with him even though I was being treated badly and gave him the impression this was acceptable. That was until I became emotionally attached to him. I'm a slag to him, so why would he treat me well or invest any time in me? Why would he want me to meet his friends, take me OUT on a date?"

"Would you have done that to him, treated him in exactly the same way he's treated you?"

"No!" There was a long pause and it hit me very hard. "No, I wouldn't hurt anyone intentionally, not ever."

"And at what point exactly did your feelings change and you told him that you loved him, or had very strong feelings for him? About a few months in. Right?"

"Yes I guess so, but I still saw other people because I didn't know what was going on, I was so confused. If he did like me then that might have upset him. That could have caused further disrespect, right?"

"So this man who you fell in love with continued to f*ck you about, for another ten months, in full knowledge that you loved him? He didn't stop it because he didn't feel the same way; he did not feel the same way, and continued to mess you about. I'm sorry but that is NOT the actions of a kind person – he's a nasty, selfish bastard of a man. I'm a man and even *I* hate him! You deserve to be with someone who loves you, someone who respects you and the rest will follow. You are intelligent and beautiful and kind. How can you be so unbelievably stupid?"

I began to cry and couldn't stop. He'd been clear and kind with his words but they'd had such an impact on me;

how could these facts be wrong? Everything that he was saying was true. 'Mr Fancy Pants' did not love me, and never had and I have spent a full year chasing after an illusion.

"How the hell do I stop loving someone?"

"I had to do this once, but although it was reciprocated love, we just couldn't be together. I had to pretend that she had died. I blocked her from my life and went into mourning. Thoughts of her still pop into my mind occasionally, but so do thoughts of my dead grandma, do you see?"

"So, I block him from my phone, my life?" I didn't want to do this, this was terrifying for me.

"Yes, and the sooner the better. Every day will be hard and the first six months will drive you insane but then you will start to forget, it won't be as intense and you will move on. I know you will text him again before you decide to move on, somehow you will get in contact with him. I did with my ex, it's normal, but when you do, I'm placing a bet!"

"OK, what is it?"

"I know you will get arrested and end up in jail if the police ever find you naked again in public. Then, next time you text him, wherever you are you take your clothes off and throw them away. That should stop you, you stupid f*cker!"

"Deal; you have my word, and I never break my word. Thank you for today, I needed someone to talk some sense into me, I still love him though."

"I know you do. It will get easier but first the pain will get worse. Have a break from dating, go see your friends and have a good time. This break you're taking now is a fantastic idea."

We both rang off and I composed myself and let the dog out of the car for him to go to the toilet. The mountains looked so beautiful, the air was so fresh and the sun's heat was just enough to keep me warm. I thought about what I'd just been told, the fact that perhaps I was as much to blame. I messed things up too, but how hard is it to realise that someone you loved with every part of you didn't love you back, that is until you're shown in black and white the reality of it?

I was overwhelmed by tears, hyperventilating and shaking; I was going into shock. I tied the dog to a bench nearby and did a search for a local pet rescue. Once I'd stopped crying, I called them to tell them I'd found a dog abandoned by the side of the road and my location. I got back into my car and faced it towards the cliff edge. The dog was barking like crazy at me and I had to completely ignore him and focus through my tears which had begun again. I put my car into first gear and pushed the accelerator to the floor, blanking my mind from anything that would stop me from doing this. I wanted to die. The pain would then go away, I wouldn't have to 'get over him' and what sort of person was I anyway? A slag, a pointless waste of life, with no prospects, who would want me, f*ck the lid for every pot, my pot's broken, and smashed up.

I closed my eyes. I heard a massive bang; this was it, I was over the edge. I stepped on my brake automatically. When I opened my eyes, I was still at the edge of the cliff, my car had stopped and a massive bird was sprawled across my windscreen. I got out and looked at the poor dead bird. I cried for a good ten minutes, so much so that I could hardly catch my breath. I looked in my car for a blanket and began to wrap the bird in it. From my observations in the past walking around Scotland with friends sightseeing I think I recognised it as a red kite, such a beautiful bird, surprisingly heavy and still warm.

I placed it in the footwell, reversed my car away from the cliff edge, put the dog back in and calmed him down with reassuring hugs and kisses. He was so pleased to see me and he licked the tears off my face.

I sat with the bird in my arms, keeping it warm, hoping it was just stunned. Staring into the distance and I thought about what I had just done. Strangely, I felt amazingly calm now, as if I'd had the most intense emotion of my life and what followed it was clarity. No situation in life will ever get me to this point again, and no man is worth this pain.

To my amazement the bird started to move. I unravelled the blanket and placed the bird down on the ground, outside the car. It struggled for a bit, looking drunk and wobbly and then spread its massive wings and flew off. I watched it fly free and wild, just like me, it was so beautiful to watch, and it made me cry again – but smile too.

I looked up into the sky and said, "OK, I get it." I sat silently for a long time, deep in thought. I realised that my life had been re-set, my path had been changed and I could feel the shift, and I knew what I had to do.

Getting back into the car my phone was going crazy, friends asking me what time I was going to arrive, and where was I? A message from the RSPCA, SHIT! I'd better get going with the dog before they realise.

To my utter surprise, I couldn't believe it; I had a text from 'Mr Pontius Pilate Not So Fancy Any More To Me Pants'.

'Hey, what you up to?' I took a few minutes to reply because I wanted this to be the last message he'd ever receive from me, the one that made him exit my life – because he had to. I knew I loved this man with every part of my soul, and doing this was the hardest thing I had ever had to do. I wanted to be with him forever, but forever for him was never his intent; sex was and I couldn't be his 'forever pussy on tap'.

'I'm sorry, Little Miss Dial A F*ck has gone ex-directory!' I waited until he had read it and then blocked him. I looked up into the sky, tears filled my eyes. My world was over, the pain was like nothing I could describe. I am more than just a fuck! I can do better than this.

Moments later I got out of the car, stripped naked and left my clothes in a heap by the side of the road. I took a photograph and sent it to 'Mr Philosopher', accompanied by the words 'Now it's over!'

Getting back into my car I lit a cigarette, being careful not to burn my naked body, asked the dog to stop staring at me and turned the radio's volume up to full. I put some red lipstick on and my shades and drove off at high speed to Tina Turner's song 'Addicted to love' blaring out. I sang it at the top of my voice, forced a smile and an attitude and told myself that everything would be OK, I can get over him, and I had an exciting new journey ahead of me, I am strong! I can do this!

An hour into the drive my phone rings off a withheld number. I pull up and answer thinking it is one of the job interviews getting back to me, grabbed a jacket from the back of the car and placed it over me.

"Hello?"

"Oi… What's with the attitude?"

TO BE CONTINUED